# The Growth and Influence of Islam

## In the Nations of Asia and Central Asia

# The Kurds

# The Growth and Influence of Islam

## IN THE NATIONS OF ASIA AND CENTRAL ASIA

Afghanistan

Azerbaijan

Bangladesh

Indonesia

Islam in Asia: Facts and Figures

Islamist Terrorism in Asia

Kazakhstan

The Kurds

Kyrgyzstan

Malaysia

Muslims in China

Muslims in India

Muslims in Russia

Pakistan

Tajikistan

Turkmenistan

Uzbekistan

# The Growth and Influence of Islam
## In the Nations of Asia and Central Asia

# The Kurds

**LeeAnne Gelletly**

**Mason Crest Publishers**
**Philadelphia**

Produced by OTTN Publishing, Stockton, New Jersey

**Mason Crest Publishers**
370 Reed Road
Broomall, PA 19008
www.masoncrest.com

First printing

1  3  5  7  9  8  6  4  2

Library of Congress Cataloging-in-Publication Data

Gelletly, LeeAnne.
 The Kurds / Leeanne Gelletly.
    p. cm. — (Growth and influence of Islam in the nations of Asia and
Central Asia)
 Includes bibliographical references and index.
 ISBN 1-59084-837-3
 1.  Kurds—Juvenile literature. 2.  Kurdistan—Juvenile literature.  I.
Title. II. Series.
 DS59.K86G45 2005
 956.6'7—dc22
                              2004019831

The Growth and Influence of Islam
IN THE NATIONS OF ASIA AND CENTRAL ASIA

# Table of Contents

This monument in Halabja, Iraq, is dediated to the victims of a chemical gas attack carried out against the town's Kurdish population in 1988. Approximately 6,000 Kurds were killed in the attack, which was ordered by Iraqi dictator Saddam Hussein.

Dr. Harvey Sicherman, president and director of the Foreign Policy Research Institute, is the author of such books as America the Vulnerable: Our Military Problems and How to Fix Them (2002) and Palestinian Autonomy, Self-Government and Peace (1993).

# Introduction

## by Dr. Harvey Sicherman

America's triumph in the Cold War promised a new burst of peace and prosperity. Indeed, the decade between the demise of the Soviet Union and the destruction of September 11, 2001, proved deceptively hopeful. Today, of course, we are more fully aware—to our sorrow—of the dangers and troubles no longer just below the surface.

The Muslim identities of most of the terrorists at war with the United States have also provoked great interest in Islam as well as the role of religion in politics. It is crucial for Americans not to assume that Osama bin Laden's ideas are identical to those of most Muslims or, for that matter, that most Muslims are Arabs. A truly world religion, Islam claims hundreds of millions of adherents, from every ethnic group scattered across the globe. This book series covers the growth and influence of Muslims in Asia and Central Asia.

A glance at the map establishes the extraordinary coverage of our authors. Every climate and terrain may be found, along with every form of human society, from the nomadic groups of the Central Asian steppes to highly sophisticated cities such as Singapore, New Delhi, and Shanghai. The economies of the nations examined in this series are likewise highly diverse. In some, barter systems are still used; others incorporate modern stock markets. In some of the countries, large oil reserves hold out the prospect of prosperity. Other countries, such as India and China, have progressed by moving from a government-controlled to a more market-based economic system. Still other countries have built wealth on service and shipping.

Central Asia and Asia is a heavily armed and turbulent area. Three of its states (China, India, and Pakistan) are nuclear powers, and one (Kazakhstan) only recently rid itself of nuclear weapons. But it is also a place where the horse and mule remain indispensable instruments of war. All of the region's states have an extensive history of conflict, domestic and international, old and new. Afghanistan, for example, has known little but invasion and civil war over the past two decades.

Governments include dictatorships, democracies, and hybrids without a name; centralized and decentralized administrations; and older patterns of tribal and clan associations. The region is a veritable encyclopedia of political expression.

Although such variety defies easy generalities, it is still possible to make several observations. First, the geopolitics of Central Asia and Asia reflect the impact of empires and the struggles of post-imperial independence. Central Asia, a historic corridor for traders and soldiers, was the scene of Russian expansion well into Soviet times. While Kazakhstan's leaders participated in the historic meeting of December 25, 1991, that dissolved the Soviet Union, the rest of the region's newly independent republics hardly expected it. They have found it difficult to grapple with a sometimes tenuous independence, buffeted by a strong residual Russian influence, the absence of settled institutions, the temptation of newly valuable natural resources, and mixed populations lacking a solid national identity. The shards of the Soviet Union have often been sharp—witness the Russian war in Chechnya—and sometimes fatal for those ambitious to grasp them.

*Peshmerga* fighters like these have fought for Kurdish independence, defended Kurds in northern Iraq after 1992, and helped U.S. forces when they invaded Iraq in the spring of 2003.

Moving further east, one encounters an older devolution, that of the half-century since the British Raj dissolved into India and Pakistan (the latter giving violent birth to Bangladesh in 1971). Only recently, partly under the impact of the war on terrorism, have these nuclear-armed neighbors and adversaries found it possible to renew attempts at reconciliation. Still further east, Malaysia shares a British experience, but Indonesia has been influenced by its Dutch heritage. Even China defines its own borders along the lines of the Qing empire (the last pre-republican dynasty) at its most expansionist (including Tibet and Taiwan). These imperial histories lie heavily upon the politics of the region.

A second aspect worth noting is the variety of economic experimentation afoot in the area. State-dominated economic strategies, still in the ascendant, are separating government from the actual running of commerce and industry. "Privatization," however, is frequently a byword for crony capitalism and corruption. Yet in dynamic economies such as that of China, as well as an increasingly productive India, hundreds of millions of people have dramatically improved both their standard of living and their hope for the future. All of them aspire to benefit from international trade. Competitive advantages, such as low-cost labor (in some cases trained in high technology) and valuable natural resources (oil, gas, and minerals), promise much. This is indeed a revolution of rising expectations, some of which are being satisfied.

Yet more than corruption threatens this progress. Population increase, even though moderating, still overwhelms educational and employment opportunities. Many countries are marked by extremes of wealth and poverty, especially between rural and urban areas. Dangerous jealousies threaten ethnic groups (such as anti-Chinese violence in Indonesia). Hopelessly overburdened public services portend turmoil. Public health, never adequate, is harmed further by environmental damage to critical resources (such as the Aral Sea). By and large, Central Asian and Asian countries are living well beyond their infrastructures.

Third and finally, Islam has deeply affected the states and peoples of the region. Indonesia is the largest Muslim state in the world, and India hosts the second-largest Muslim population. Islam is not only the official religion of many states, it is the very reason for Pakistan's existence. But Islamic practices and groups vary: the well-known Sunni and Shiite groups are joined by energetic Salafi (Wahabi) and Sufi movements. Over the last 20 years especially, South and Central Asia have become battle-grounds for competing Shiite (Iranian) and Wahabi (Saudi) doctrines, well financed from abroad and aggressively antagonistic toward non-Muslims and each other. Resistance to the Soviet invasion of Afghanistan brought these groups battle-tested warriors and organizers. The war on terrorism has exposed just how far-reaching and active the new advocates of holy war (jihad) can be. Indonesia, in particular, is the scene of rivalry between an older, tolerant Islam and the jihadists. But Pakistan also faces an Islamic identity crisis. And India, wracked by sectarian strife, must hold together its democratic framework despite Muslim and Hindu extremists. This newly significant struggle within Islam, superimposed on an older Muslim history, will shape political and economic destinies throughout the region and beyond. Hence, the focus of our series.

We hope that these books will enlighten both teacher and student about a critical subject in a critical area of the world. Central Asia and Asia would be important in their own right to Americans; arguably, after 9/11, they became vital to our national security. And the enduring impact of Islam is a crucial factor we must understand. We at the Foreign Policy Research Institute hope these books will illuminate both the facts and the prospects.

Iraqi Kurds wave their national flag during an October 2004 demonstration in Kirkuk calling for Iraqi Kurdistan to become a separate state. Kurds are considered the largest ethnic group without a state of their own. Although some Kurds would like to have an independent country, others prefer greater freedom within the nation where they now live.

# 1

# *Place in the World*

In the mountainous regions of Southwest Asia and the Middle East lives the largest **ethnic** group without a nation of its own—the Kurdish people. The Kurds number more than 25 million, which makes them the fourth-largest ethnic faction in the region (after Arabs, Persians, and Turks). Yet the land they consider their ancestral homeland—Kurdistan—is not recognized by the rest of the world as a separate, independent state. Instead, most of Kurdistan, which is Arabic for "land of the Kurds," is divided up among several nations, including Turkey, Iraq, Syria, and Iran.

More than half of the estimated Kurdish population (around 13 to 14 million people) live in Turkey.

Around 5 to 7 million Kurds live in Iran, 4 to 5 million live in Iraq, and 1.5 million live in Syria. Smaller numbers can be found living in parts of the former Soviet Union (Armenia, Azerbaijan, Georgia, Turkmenistan, and Kazakhstan), while an estimated 5 million Kurds have left the region and settled in other countries, including the United States, Germany, France, and Sweden.

## Who Are the Kurds?

The Kurds are an ancient people who can trace their history back for thousands of years. For centuries they lived as **nomads** in the mountains of Southwest Asia, migrating with the seasons to find pastureland for their herds of livestock. In the summer, Kurdish shepherds would drive their flocks of sheep and goats into the high mountain peaks and **plateaus** of Kurdistan, while in the winter they would bring the flocks and herds down to graze in the lowlands. Since around the seventh century, the word *Kurd* has meant "nomad."

Most Kurds belonged to clans, tribes, and tribal confederations that claimed rights to or ownership of the land used during these seasonal migrations. Almost 800 different tribes and subtribes can be found in Kurdistan, many with their own distinct dress, music, and folklore. However, today few Kurds are nomadic. Most are farmers who have settled in villages and towns. And some have migrated to the cities in search of jobs.

Kurds speak their own language, Kurdish. However, because the language exists in a variety of dialects, people from different parts of Kurdistan sometimes cannot understand one another. Most follow the **Sunni** Muslim faith, but their loyalties to their clans and tribal chiefs have been known to take precedence over their religious ties.

The Kurds are a fiercely independent mountain people who take great pride in their history, culture, and traditions.

# The Kurdish Question

Although the Kurds' mountainous homeland never officially existed as a nation, during the late 19th century maps of Southwest Asia often identified the region of Kurdistan. After World War I (1914–18), Kurdistan stopped appearing on official maps as postwar settlements resulted in the division of Kurdish land among the modern-day nations of Turkey, Iraq, Iran, Syria, and the Soviet Union. In each nation, despite their large numbers the Kurds became a minority ethnic group.

Many Kurds did not want to be a part of another nation. The newly imposed borders separated Kurdish tribes and even families. As the new nations enforced their boundaries, tribes could no longer easily travel from one part of Kurdistan to another, and these restrictions disrupted their traditional, nomadic way of life.

In addition, the new governments often refused to acknowledge the Kurds as a separate ethnic group, or they treated them as second-class citizens by withholding basic civil and political rights. In some cases the Kurds' native language—in spoken and written form—was outlawed. Kurds were often not allowed to vote, own property, or receive an education in their own language. As a result of this repression, many Kurds found themselves shackled to a life of extreme poverty.

As the Kurdish people chafed under oppressive rule, some dreamt of forming their own separate Kurdish nation. Kurdish uprisings began in 1919, even before Kurdistan was officially divided among the four nations of Turkey, Iraq, Iran, and Syria. However, the governments of these countries quickly repressed any instances of unrest through legislation and force. In the face of government opposition, resistance continued throughout the rest of the 20th century as Kurds sporadically rose up against the authorities of their respective governments.

Most rebellions were short-lived but had serious repercussions. They often resulted in further persecution, as well as death, for hundreds of thousands of Kurds. Kurdish independence fighters, or ***peshmerga*** ("those who face death"), and civilians suffered dearly from decades of fighting to achieve an unfulfilled dream. It was not until 1992 that the Kurds of Iraq finally managed to create a form of self-rule, although as a government that was still part of the nation of Iraq.

In the spring of 1991, shortly after the defeat of Iraq during the first Persian Gulf War, the United States had encouraged the Kurds to rise up against the government of Saddam Hussein. However, the U.S. government did not help the Kurdish rebels, and Saddam crushed the rebellion swiftly and brutally. Hundreds of thousands of surviving Kurds fled for safety to Turkey, while many others found themselves stranded in the high mountains of Iraq. During the bitter cold months of winter they struggled for survival, as television images and newspaper stories shared the Kurds' plight with the rest of the world. Soon the United States, France, and Great Britain agreed to help the Kurds by setting up a protected zone in northern

Iraq. Within this safe haven, dubbed "Iraqi Kurdistan," the Kurds of Iraq soon developed their own ***autonomous*** government.

In Turkey, Kurds make up about 20 percent of the population; in Syria, they make up 8 percent; and in Iran, 7 percent. The governments of these three nations raised concerns about the new Iraqi Kurdistan. They viewed the establishment of a separate Kurdish nation in Iraq as a threat to their own stability, because an independent Kurdish state could inspire their minority Kurdish populations to rebel.

It is true that for close to a century, the Kurds' desire for self-rule has led to instability and violence in the Middle East region. But the Kurds have been fighting for freedoms they have been denied for decades. Some do not see the need for the establishment of a separate Kurdish nation, but simply want the right to practice their own traditions and culture where they live.

After living for 12 years within their autonomous government, Iraqi Kurds, who make up 15 to 20 percent of Iraq's population, continue to seek political and cultural rights. This issue became volatile following the second Persian Gulf War in 2003, as the future of the nation of Iraq remained uncertain. The issue of Kurdish autonomy—whether as a region within an existing nation or as a wholly independent state—remains a source of conflict and political tension in this part of the world.

A view of the mountains of Iraqi Kurdistan near Dahuk. The region historically known as Kurdistan actually stretches across the borders of several modern-day states, including Turkey, Iraq, Iran, and Syria.

# 2

# The Land

Because Kurdistan is not recognized by the rest of the world as a nation, its geographical boundaries have never been officially defined. Mapmakers usually indicate the area as the lands containing a majority Kurdish population.

The region known as Kurdistan encompasses parts of eastern Turkey, northeastern Iraq, northwestern Iran, and small portions of Syria, as well as parts of the former Soviet Union. The vast tract is shaped somewhat like a wide-angled upside-down *V*, with the point of the letter directed toward the Caucasus Mountains of Armenia and Georgia. One arm of the *V* reaches southwest toward the Mediterranean Sea; the other stretches southeast toward the Persian Gulf.

Estimates of Kurdistan's size vary from as small as 74,000 square miles (191,660 sq km, or about the size of the state of Washington) to as large as 230,000 square miles (595,700 sq km, or slightly smaller than Texas).

## Land of Mountains

Kurdistan contains numerous rugged mountains, deep-cut river gorges, sheer rock cliffs, and high plateaus. Its major mountain ranges include the central and northern Zagros of Iran and Iraq, the Elburz (also called Alborz) of Iran, and the eastern third of the Taurus and Pontus of Turkey.

The Zagros mountain system dominates the southeastern part of Kurdistan. This extremely rugged range runs southeast from northern Iraq along the western border of Iran toward the Persian Gulf. Many of its lofty peaks reach higher than 10,000 feet (3,048 meters) and at such great altitudes remain snowcapped year-round. The tallest peak of the Zagros range, called Zard Kuh (or Zardeh Kuh), rises 14,921 feet (4,548 meters) above sea level.

Also in southeastern Kurdistan are the Elburz Mountains, which extend for almost 620 miles (998 km) along the northern border of Iran, just south of the Caspian Sea. In the center of these jagged mountains lies their highest peak, as well as the highest point in Iran—Mount Damavand. A dormant volcano, Mount Damavand rises 18,606 feet (5,671 meters) high. The Elburz range stretches into northeastern Kurdistan, where it meets the highlands and plateaus of the eastern half of the Taurus Mountains. Sometimes the mountains in this area are referred to as the Ararat Mountains. Here, near the border with Armenia and Iran, sits the extinct volcano that is Turkey's highest peak. Mount Ararat, thought by some biblical scholars to be the resting place of Noah's ark after the Great Flood, stands 16,949 feet (5,166 meters) high.

In western Kurdistan the mountains give way to the lower elevations and rolling hills of Turkey's eastern Anatolian Plateau, which average

1,640 feet (500 meters) above sea level. Toward the south, in the direction of Syria, the mountains descend to the dry **steppes** and flat plains of northern Mesopotamia.

Mesopotamia refers to the ancient region said to be the site of the first human civilization. The word *Mesopotamia* is of Greek origin, and means "land between the rivers." Mesopotamia is embraced by two major rivers of the Middle East—the Tigris (Diçle, in Kurdish) and Euphrates. These two rivers, both important sources of irrigation for Syria, Turkey, and Iraq, originate in Kurdistan and flow southeast until they meet in southeastern Iraq and empty into the Persian Gulf.

The northern plains of Mesopotamia include a fertile region known as al-Jazirah, which is Arabic for "the island." For many centuries al-Jazirah served as a huge grazing ground used by the flocks of both Arab and Kurdish nomads. Later it was settled by many Kurds, who farmed the land and helped make it become a major agricultural region, or "breadbasket," of the Middle East.

## An Abundance of Water

Unlike much of the rest of the Middle East, which has little rainfall, Kurdistan can boast of an abundance of water. Numerous rivers rush through the valleys and gorges of the region. Some, such as the Khabur, Tharthar, Ceyhan, Araks, and Kura, have their headwaters in Kurdistan's mountains, but flow mostly outside of Kurdistan's borders. Other rivers

The "Fertile Crescent," the richest farmland of the Middle East, lies within Kurdistan. The productive agricultural region extends from the eastern shore of the Mediterranean Sea, through the Zagros mountain range of Iran and Iraq, to the Persian Gulf.

> **About one-half of Kurdistan, in terms of population and size, can be found within the borders of Turkey.**

flow mainly within Kurdistan, and are a part of the history, culture, and folklore of the Kurds. Among these significant waterways are the Mura and Buhtan Rivers of northern and western Kurdistan (Turkey); the Peshkhabur, the Lesser Zab, the Greater Zab, and the Diyala in central Kurdistan (Iraq); and the Jaghatu, the Tata'u, the Zohab, and the Gamasiyab in southern Kurdistan (Iran).

Besides supplying water for crop irrigation, Kurdistan's rivers have also been harnessed for hydroelectric projects and other industrial uses. The nations of Turkey and Iraq have built huge dams and irrigation projects along the rivers of Kurdistan, often with little concern for the economic consequences that the Kurds living in the region face. Historically, Kurds have had no control over the development of such projects and often have reaped little benefit from them. Fearing a negative impact on the environment and concerned about the flooding of mountain valleys, villages, and ancient historical sites, Kurds as well as other groups have protested dam constructions along Kurdistan's rivers.

One of the most aggressive and controversial dam projects is being built by Turkey. Called the Southeast Anatolia Development Project, or GAP, this $30-billion development plan involves the construction of 22 dams and 19 hydroelectric plants on the Tigris and Euphrates Rivers. Proponents assert that GAP will provide irrigation of arid lands in southeastern Anatolia that will enable millions of Kurdish residents to make a better living. GAP opponents believe the overall venture threatens to destroy the way of life for many Kurds. For example, they claim that when the Ilisu Dam is built it will flood 100 Kurdish villages and destroy the archaeological site of Hasankeyf, an ancient city that dates back at least 5,000 years. When completed, the Southeast Anatolia Development Project will displace more than 70,000 Kurds. Syria and Iraq have protested GAP because it will reduce the water they receive from the Tigris and Euphrates Rivers.

**The abandoned Kurdish village of Belkis sits below the Birecik dam on the Euphrates River. The dam, built as part of the Southeast Anatolia Project, will flood numerous villages and archaeological sites. It is estimated that approximately 70,000 Kurds will be displaced by the time the project is complete.**

# The Geography of Kurdistan

**Location:** Middle East and Southwestern Asia, consisting of parts of eastern Turkey, northeastern Iraq, northwestern Iran, and small portions of Syria, Armenia, Azerbaijan, Turkmenistan, and Kazakhstan

**Area:** (at largest estimate, slightly smaller than Texas) 230,000 square miles (595,700 sq km)

**Unofficial borders:** Turkey, Syria, Iraq, Iran, Armenia, Azerbaijan, Georgia, Turkmenistan, and Kazakhstan

**Climate:** harsh winters with heavy precipitation; dry summers range from hot to temperate, depending on the elevation

**Terrain:** Mostly mountain ranges and plateaus

**Elevation extremes:**
  **lowest point:** Kifri (town in northern Iraq), 544 feet (166 meters) above sea level
  **highest point:** Mount Damavand, 18,606 feet (5,671 meters), in Iran

**Natural hazards:** periodic droughts in southern Kurdistan, earthquakes

Sources: Adapted from CIA World Factbook, 2004; Kurdistan Regional Government website (www.krg.org).

The inhabitants of Kurdistan cannot look to the region's largest lakes for drinkable water, as the two largest bodies of water are quite salty. In northwest Iran lies the largest salt lake in the Middle East, a shallow body of water known as Lake Urmia. It covers 1,815 square miles (4,701 sq km), reaching a length of about 90 miles (140 km) and a width of 50 miles (80 km), though its deepest depth is just 49 feet (15 meters). The Middle East's second-largest salt lake is Lake Van, located in eastern Turkey near the border with Iran. Lake Van covers 1,434 square miles (3,713 sq km) and reaches more than 74 miles (119 km) at its widest point.

## A Fertile Land

Many people live in the river valleys, foothills, and rolling plains of Kurdistan, where the abundance of water from rivers, tributaries, and springs has combined with deep, fertile soil to support a variety of crops. About 28 percent of Kurdistan is *arable*, or suitable for cultivation. Farmers grow wheat and other grains, maintain orchards and vineyards, and raise livestock along the northern slopes of the Elburz Mountains, in the Mus Valley basin (west of Lake Van), and in the wide valleys of northern and central parts of the Zagros Mountains. Areas that do not support crops, such as the higher mountain regions, provide rich pastureland for the grazing of sheep and goats.

## Climate Extremes

Kurdistan's climate ranges from the extremes of hot, dry summers to severe, bitterly cold winters. At high altitudes heavy snowfalls can occur for a period of up to six months, leaving mountain villages isolated from December to February. Temperatures can fall as low as –20° Fahrenheit (–7° Celsius) in the winter. At the lower elevations of the river valleys, the winter climate is somewhat milder, although it can still be bitterly cold in the lower altitudes of Turkey's Anatolian plateau.

During the summer months, the daytime temperatures become hotter at low elevations than they are in the mountains. At low altitudes, summer temperatures can easily reach above 100°F (38°C), while averaging a mild 68°F (20°C) higher up. In Diyarbakir, the largest Kurdish city in Turkey, the average temperature is 86°F (30°C) in August and 23°F (–5°C) in January.

Kurdistan's many rivers are fed by large amounts of precipitation, much of which falls as snow between November and April, and then melts in the spring. Precipitation is greatest in central Kurdistan, which averages about 60 to 80 inches (150 to 200 cm) per year. The lower elevations of western Kurdistan, where steppes dominate, receive much less precipitation, averaging 20 to 40 inches (50 to 102 cm) per year. In the Kurdish region of Iraq, dry summers are often accompanied by a hot, dusty northwesterly wind called the *shamal*. This area also suffers from periodic droughts.

## Flora and Fauna

A hundred years ago, large stands of ancient oak forests covered much of Kurdistan. However, few large trees remain today. Over the years, much of the region's forest cover was cut down to build houses or for firewood. Within the past few decades many large trees were destroyed by warfare. This has sometimes been done purposely by the governments of Turkey, Iran, Iraq, and Syria, so the forests would not provide cover for Kurdish *peshmerga* fighters.

Today, twisted scrub oaks make up much of the remaining forestland in Kurdistan, although some forests may also contain cedars, chestnuts, junipers, poplars, pines, and wild fruit trees. In some wooded areas, Kurds harvest crops that have sprung up in the wild, such as fruits (grapes, cherries, and pears), berries (mulberries and blackberries), and nuts (hazelnuts, walnuts, chestnuts, and almonds).

Wildflowers are perhaps the best-known flora of Kurdistan. Flowers like the white *nergiz* (narcissus); purple, yellow, and red *sheqayiq* (ranunculus); and red *gulale* (poppy) blanket the mountainsides in the springtime and early summer. In ancient times the sheep and goats feeding on these sweet-smelling flowers produced delicious milk. According to legend, the butter made from this milk brought Vikings all the way from Scandinavia to buy it.

The forests and rivers also provide ample nourishment for the fauna of Kurdistan, which include wild black and brown bears, boars, beavers, cheetahs, hyenas, leopards, and wolves. Fish such as carp and trout abound in the region's freshwater lakes and rivers. Among Kurdistan's many native birds are bluebirds, eagles, larks, quail, and partridges. Some Kurdish families keep the *kau,* a gray bird of the partridge family, as a pet so they can enjoy its melodic song.

## Earthquakes

Kurdistan sees frequent earthquake activity, as it is located within the Alpide seismic belt, an area that has seen some of the world's most destructive earthquakes. Kurdish folk tales and legends tell of entire villages being swallowed up. Considering just how unstable the earth in this region is, it is possible these stories are largely true. Lava flows have created natural dams that have blocked river channels, forming vast lakes such as Urmia and Van.

An armed guard stands on the roof of a Baghdad office building belonging to the Patriotic Union of Kurdistan (PUK). In Iraq, two groups have fought for supremacy in Iraqi Kurdistan, the PUK and the rival Kurdistan Democratic Party (KDP).

الاتحاد الوطني الكردستاني

# 3

# The History

An ancient people, the Kurds are thought to have descended from Indo-European tribes of central Asia that moved westwards across Iran around 1500 B.C. Eventually, these groups made the Zagros and Taurus Mountains their homeland. Written records dating from the seventh century B.C. contain the first mention of Kurdish people, indicating they lived in the southern region of Lake Van, in present-day Turkey. The Greek general and historian Xenophon, who lived around 400 B.C., also described a people who most likely were Kurds. According to his writings, the Karduchoi, as they were called, were fierce fighters.

Although the mountainous lands where they lived changed hands many times as empires rose and fell (among the rulers were the Sumerians, Akkadians, Babylonians, Assyrians, Parthians, Persians, Romans, and Armenians), the Kurds did not change much in their way of life. They considered their tribal leaders the ultimate authority, not the imperial government that ruled them. Self-governing Kurdish tribal communities would pay tribute to the ruling regime, but the independent-minded Kurds mostly maintained their nomadic lifestyle as they tended their flocks and herds.

## Islamic Empires

While many things remained the same for the Kurds under foreign powers, their religious faith did not. During the seventh century A.D. Arab peoples gained control of Kurdistan and brought with them a new religion known as Islam. Founded by the prophet Muhammad, who was born around A.D. 570, Islam holds that there is only one God, called Allah. Muslims—followers of the Islamic faith—believe that the word of Allah was revealed to Muhammad, who then taught it to his followers. Later, those teachings were collected into the **Qur'an,** the holy book of Islam.

Upon Muhammad's death in 632, the Muslim community split into two factions. One group, the **Shiites,** believed that Muhammad's son-in-law Ali was the prophet's heir and the rightful leader of Islam. The name of this religious group comes from the Arabic phrase *shiat Ali,* which means "the party of Ali." A second group, the Sunnis, believed that the spiritual and political rulers of the Islamic state, or **caliphs,** should be chosen by consensus. The name *Sunni* derives from the Arabic word *Sunna,* which means "tradition." Sunni Muslims believe they are the true followers of the traditions of Muhammad and his community. They grew to become the dominant faction of Islam.

During the 600s, Islam spread quickly as Muslim Arabs conquered the lands of modern-day Egypt, Syria, and Iraq. By A.D. 711 Arab Islamic empires reached from present-day Spain to Iran. As the lands of the Kurds came under Islamic rule, most Kurdish people converted to the Sunni Muslim faith. However, they did not adopt the Arabic language.

Over the centuries many Kurdish tribes formed military groups that fought for various Islamic empires. Most Kurds today take special pride in their famous ancestor Salah ad-Din Yusuf ibn Ayyub, known to the Western world as Saladin. He was a Kurdish military leader who in the late 12th century united the Muslim lands of Syria, northern Mesopotamia (Iraq), Kurdistan, Palestine, and Egypt. In 1187, he led a Muslim army that recaptured Jerusalem and other cities from European Christians, who had conquered the region during the First **Crusade** in 1096–99. To many

**The Muslim conqueror Salah ad-Din (known in the West as Saladin) accepts the surrender of Jerusalem in 1187 by the descendants of European Crusaders who had captured the city nearly a century earlier. Most Muslims consider Salah ad-Din a hero, but he is particularly revered by Kurds.**

Tikrit, Iraq, is the birthplace of one of the Kurds' most beloved political figures, the 12th-century military leader Saladin. It is also the birthplace of one of their most hated: Iraqi dictator Saddam Hussein, who before his removal in April 2003 was responsible for the deaths of hundreds of thousands of Kurds.

Kurds Saladin is a national hero and a renowned champion of Islam, celebrated for liberating Muslim lands from the Europeans.

Although descendants of Saladin ruled his Ayyubid Empire for several generations following his death, after the empire fell the Mongols from Central Asia took control of Kurdish lands. The region was important, because Kurdistan was a part of the Silk Road, a series of trade routes that linked Asia with Europe. Merchants and traders traveling the Silk Road also purchased Kurdish handicrafts, particularly the region's famous woven rugs.

## *The Ottoman Empire*

The 14th century saw the rise of the Ottoman empire, named for its first *sultan*, Osman I. During the 1300s and 1400s Ottoman forces swept across the Anatolian plateau. In 1453, they captured the city of Constantinople, bringing to an end the powerful Byzantine empire. The Ottomans renamed the city Istanbul and made it their capital. After the conquest of the Byzantines, the Ottoman empire became the strongest power in the region, conquering and controlling vast territories. At its peak in the 16th and 17th centuries, the kingdom included not only Kurdistan and Mesopotamia but also lands in present-day northern Africa and southeastern Europe.

For centuries, the majority of Kurds lived under the rule of the Ottoman sultans, although some Kurdish people were governed by Persian *shahs* of the Safavid empire (1501–1722). This empire, which was ruled by Shiite Muslims, controlled lands east of the Ottoman empire, including the area of modern-day Iran.

In both the Ottoman and the Safavid empires, Kurdish princes governed tribal communities, or emirates. Sultans and shahs gave the princes semi-autonomous powers in return for paying tribute or providing Kurdish fighters to the empire. In the Kurdish areas within the Ottoman empire (particularly

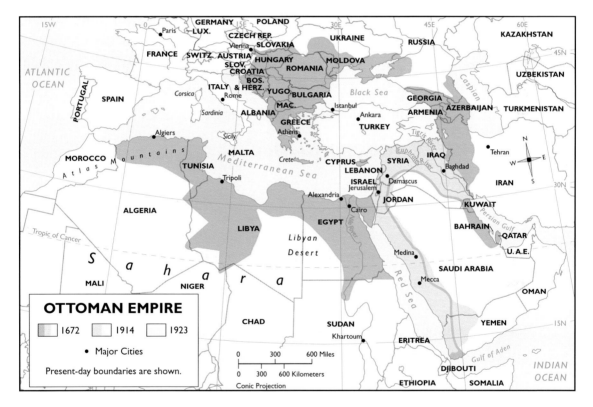

**After conquering Constantinople in 1453, the Ottoman Empire continued to expand its boundaries during the 15th and 16th centuries. The empire reached its height in 1672, when it controlled much of the Middle East as well as large parts of north Africa, central Asia, and eastern Europe. Although the empire had lost much of its territory by the start of World War I (1914) it still included most of Kurdistan. After the war, the modern state of Turkey was established by the Treaty of Lausanne (1923), and control over Kurdistan and other former Ottoman territories was divided among the victorious allied powers.**

present-day Iraq and Turkey) there were 16 large emirates (such as Bahdinan, Soran, and Baban) and approximately 50 Kurdish fiefdoms, or smaller kingdoms. The courts in these principalities featured much learning, with poets, scientists, and religious scholars held in high esteem.

During the 19th century, some Kurdish princes began to fight against the Ottoman empire for independence. At the same time, the empire was weakening just as several European nations were growing stronger. In 1914, Sultan Muhammad VI brought the Ottoman empire into World War I on the side of Germany and against the alliance of France, Italy, Russia, and the United Kingdom. After Germany's defeat in 1918, the victorious Allies divided the lands of the Ottoman empire. The Kurdish people awaited the partitioning eagerly, for they had been promised that the region known as Kurdistan would officially be made a separate nation.

## *Promise of Independence*

The Treaty of Sevres, signed in 1920 by the Ottoman sultan and representatives of the triumphant European countries, called for the establishment of a Kurdish state. However, that independent nation was never realized.

Although the Ottoman sultan had surrendered, one of his generals would not. Mustafa Kemal (more popularly known as Mustafa Atatürk, the name he later took as president) refused to submit to the demands of the Treaty of Sevres, and he inspired the Turkish military forces under his command to continue fighting. Their victories forced the Allies to renegotiate the Sevres peace treaty, which in 1923 was replaced by the Treaty of Lausanne. The latter agreement created the independent nation that the Turkish general wanted. Called the Republic of Turkey, the newly created country had boundaries that cut deeply into northern Kurdistan.

The League of Nations, an international organization created after World War I to promote worldwide peace and security, authorized France and Britain to rule newly created Middle East territories as **mandates**.

France received a mandate to rule Syria, which included part of southern Kurdistan. Great Britain controlled Mesopotamia, renamed Iraq, which was created from the Ottoman *vilayets*, or provinces, of Baghdad, Basra, and Mosul. (The Kurds considered—and still consider—the oil-rich Mosul region part of southern Kurdistan.)

As a result of the Treaty of Lausanne, the Kurdish people had become minority groups in three different nations: Turkey, Iraq, and Syria. Those living in Persia had been a minority since the 1500s.

## A Minority in Turkey

Following its official creation in 1923, Turkey worked to impose unity on the population within its boundaries. The country would meet this objective, government leaders believed, by refusing to acknowledge that separate ethnic groups even existed. Everyone was a Turk according to President Atatürk (whose name, which means "the father of all Turks," reflected his unifying mission). Subsequently, the Kurds were deemed "mountain Turks" who had forgotten their language.

The government refused to recognize Kurdish linguistic or cultural rights. Turkish laws prohibited Kurds from speaking their native language in public, teaching or publishing in the Kurdish language, or using Kurdish in the courts or government offices. Even the word *Kurdistan* was removed from official documents. The new Turkish state established a centralized taxation system on Kurdish lands, effectively taking away the Kurds' financial autonomy. Atatürk abolished the Muslim caliphate as well, an action that angered many religious Kurds.

As their cultural, economic, and religious rights were taken away, the Kurds revolted in 1925 under the leadership of Sheikh Said Piran. His forces were quickly crushed. Subsequent uprisings during the 1930s were similarly put down, as thousands of Kurds were killed and as many as a million lost their homes to bombings.

**A painting of Mustafa Kemal Atatürk (1881–1938), the founder of modern Turkey. After the end of World War I Atatürk led Turkey to independence, but this came at the expense of the Kurds, who had initially been promised a separate state by the Treaty of Sevres. As president of Turkey, Atatürk refused to officially admit that the Kurds were a separate ethnic group, and Kurds lost their cultural and economic rights in the new state.**

In the decades that followed, few Kurds made an attempt to revive a Kurdish nationalist movement. It was not until 1978 that student activist Abdullah Öcalan founded the Kurdish Workers' Party (Partiya Karkere Kurdistan, or PKK). The party advocated for a completely independent Kurdish state, and sought this goal by any means possible. In 1984, open warfare broke out between Turkish government forces and the PKK in various parts of southeastern Turkey. As leader of the PKK, Öcalan directed the attacks and battle operations from his base in Syria.

Soon the PKK engaged in violence not only against Turkish troops, but against anyone identified as a government collaborator. Targets included schoolteachers (for forcing the Turkish language upon Kurds) and government workers such as police officers, state officials, and village guards. The PKK struck not only in southeastern Turkey but also in its western cities and in other European nations. Although several countries, including Turkey and the United States, identified the PKK as a terrorist organization, it continued to find a large following among Kurdish residents of Turkey who resented the Turkish government's oppression.

The Turkish government responded to the PKK attacks by establishing state-of-emergency rule, or **martial law,** in southeastern Turkey and bringing in approximately 220,000 Turkish troops. Many Kurds suffered under emergency rule, which permitted authorities to hold suspects in confinement for 30 days, as well as deny them the right to an appeal. In 1992, convinced that the Kurds living in the southeastern region were sympathetic to the PKK rebels, Turkish government forces emptied and burned thousands of villages, many along the border with Iraq. Military troops, gunships, and helicopters forcibly evicted Kurds from their mountain farmlands. An estimated 3 million refugees fled to the Kurdish city of Diyarbakir and even further to the western Turkish cities of Ankara and Istanbul.

**Kurdish demonstrators in Istanbul hold banners supporting imprisoned rebel leader Abdullah Öcalan, founder of the PKK.**

During the early 1990s, Turkish President Turgut Özal urged the government to address the Kurdish issue. Eager to institute reforms, Özal acknowledged that Kurds were a separate ethnic group. He promoted changes in the laws to permit Kurdish song, speech, and music, although the use of Kurdish in the courts, in schools, and in radio and television broadcasts remained prohibited. However, his sudden death in 1993 from a heart attack prevented Turkey from making further progress in granting Kurdish rights.

PKK rebels operated from bases in Syria and Iraq, just across the border, so they could strike in rural southeastern Turkey and then retreat to safety. In 1995 and again in 1996 Turkish troops crossed the border into northern Iraq to attack PKK bases there.

Finally, in 1999 hostilities between the PKK and the Turkish government ended with the capture of Öcalan (he is now serving a sentence of life imprisonment). Soon after, the PKK agreed to a ceasefire. In April 2002 it renamed itself the Kurdish Congress for Freedom and Democracy, or KADEK, and announced it no longer supported the creation of an independent Kurdish state, but instead sought the establishment of an autonomous Kurdish territory within Turkey and the recognition of Kurds' rights.

The years of warfare took a severe toll on the Kurds of Turkey. During that time, human rights organizations documented assassinations, disappearances, firebombing of homes, and torture by police. Human Rights Watch estimated that more than 3,000 Kurdish villages in Turkey were destroyed between 1984 and 1994, and more than 250,000 Kurds were made homeless. More than 30,000 people—military personnel and civilians—lost their lives as a result of the conflicts between the PKK and Turkish government.

In 2002 and 2003, under pressure from European nations, Turkish legislators began passing some human rights reforms. New laws ended bans on teaching Kurdish and giving children Kurdish names. They also allowed for state television and radio stations to broadcast in Kurdish. Around the same time the state of emergency in place in most of southeastern Turkey was lifted, and many rural Kurds were allowed to return to their villages. Tensions between the Kurds and the Turkish government remain, although few today openly support a completely independent Kurdish state.

## *A Minority in Iraq*

The Kurds of Iraq rebelled first against the British mandate and later against the constitutional monarchy of Emir Faisal, whom the British placed on the throne in 1932 and continued to support militarily. In 1919, 1922, and 1923 Sheikh Mahmoud Barzinji led several unsuccessful Kurdish uprisings. They were followed in 1932 by a rebellion led by Mulla Mustafa Barzani and his older brother, Ahmad. Although Mustafa's uprising was also crushed, the Kurdish leader would persist for 40 more years as he waged campaigns for a separate Kurdish state and earned the appreciation and love of his people.

In 1943 Barzani's Kurdish forces captured regions around the cities of Arbil and Badinan, but British warplanes pushed his *peshmerga* militia out of Iraq and into Iran. There Barzani's forces joined with rebellious Iranian Kurds and in 1946 declared an independent Kurdish state called the Mahabad Republic. Supported by the Soviet Union and administered by the newly established Kurdistan Democratic Party (KDP), the Mahabad Republic lasted for less than a year and then collapsed. Barzani, who had served as commander-in-chief of the short-lived government, fled to the Soviet Union.

During the next decade, the KDP regained strength in Iraq. In 1958, the Iraqi monarchy was overthrown by a group of military officers led by General Abd al-Karim Qasim. Believing that the coup signaled positive change, Mulla Mustafa returned from exile. The future looked promising: a

**Rival Kurdish leaders Massoud Barzani (right) of the KDP and Jalal Talabani of the PUK stand together in front of a painting of Mustafa Barzani, the father of Kurdish nationalism in Iraq.**

new Iraqi constitution promised national rights for Kurds, now considered a part of the new Iraqi state; they were allowed to broadcast and publish in Kurdish; and they could attend Kurdish schools ranging from the elementary to the university level.

However, although Iraq was called a republic it was effectively run by a series of dictators who rejected the idea of granting autonomy to the Kurds. By 1961 the KDP had been banned, and Kurds under the leadership of Mulla Mustafa were battling the government. Fighting did not end until March 1970, when the Kurds were granted rights in a peace accord signed by Barzani and Saddam Hussein, then the vice president of the Baath Party, which had come into power in 1968.

In March 1974, Iraqi president Ahmed Hasan al-Bakr released an official proclamation defining Iraqi Kurdistan as an autonomous province within Iraq, with Arbil as its capital. The announcement established an elected legislative assembly and executive council, and identified Kurdish as one of Iraq's official languages. However, the plan had several points that the Kurds disputed. Barzani, who had become leader of the Kurdistan Democratic Party, rejected the proposal because it failed to include half of what the Kurds considered their land, including the oil-rich region around the city of Kirkuk. It also did not provide an adequate share of oil revenues, or allow for fair Kurdish representation in the Iraqi government.

Civil war resumed in March 1974, with Iran, Israel, and the United States providing the Kurds with much-needed support. However, a year later these countries withdrew their backing. The Kurdish uprising in Iraq collapsed, and, fearing a severe reprisal by the Iraqi Baathist government, more than 100,000 Kurds fled to Iran. Thousands who remained were killed by Iraqi forces. Barzani fled to the United States, where he died in 1979.

Dissent within the KDP resulted in the creation of a new political party. In 1975 former KDP member Jalal Talabani founded the Patriotic Union of Kurdistan (PUK). The group soon clashed with the KDP, led by Mustafa's son, Massoud Barzani.

Meanwhile, the ruling Baath party began instituting policies to acquire greater control of the oil in Kurdish territory. In the mid-1970s the government implemented the policy of "Arabization" of oil-rich Kurdish areas, particularly in Kirkuk and Khanaqin. To transform the populations in these regions from predominantly Kurdish to Arab, government troops evicted Kurdish farmers and replaced them with Arab tribesmen. More than half of Iraq's Kurds would be displaced. Around the same time the government forbid any teaching in Kurdish and closed Kurdish schools and universities.

In 1979 al-Bakr resigned the Iraqi presidency, and the Baathist regime continued under Saddam Hussein, who ruled as dictator. One of his first major actions as president was to invade Iraq's longtime enemy, Iran, in 1980. The Kurds became embroiled in the ensuing eight-year-long conflict, as both countries contended for Kurdish territory in northern Iraq. The Kurds sided with Iran against the Baghdad government, and they paid dearly for their allegiance. In 1983 all Iraqi Kurdish villages within 12.5 miles (20 km) of the Iranian border were destroyed as Saddam Hussein's forces moved their inhabitants into "collective towns," located in army-controlled areas of northern Iraq. Some Kurds were relocated to barren desert towns in southern Iraq, while thousands of male Kurds over the age of 12 simply disappeared. It was later learned that they had been rounded up, executed, and buried in mass graves.

The lack of international outcry over this massacre led to further atrocities. In 1988, from February 23 until September 6, the Iraqi *Anfal* military campaign led by Ali Hassan al-Majid killed thousands of Kurds. Later nicknamed "Chemical Ali," al-Majid had clearance to use chemical weapons to kill thousands of Kurdish men, women, and children. His goal, in his own words, was "to solve the Kurdish problem and slaughter the saboteurs." To accomplish this, his men systematically destroyed approximately 1,200 Kurdish villages by bulldozing the buildings, covering wells and springs with concrete, and poisoning the fields.

In the village of Halabja alone, approximately 6,000 Kurds were massacred by poison gas dropped by Iraqi government bombs in 1988. Thousands more Kurds were rounded up and sent to refugee camps, where they received no food, water, or shelter (they survived only because of secret help from nearby residents). As many as 180,000 men were executed and their bodies bulldozed into mass graves.

In August 1990, Iraq invaded its neighbor to the south, Kuwait. In response, a coalition of 34 nations, including the United States, went to war against the Iraqi government of Saddam Hussein. Begun in mid-January 1991, the first Persian Gulf War ended at the end of February with the expulsion of Iraqi forces from Kuwait.

Soon after, in March 1991, the Kurds once again rose up against the Iraqi government. However, the *peshmerga* forces received little support from the allied coalition, and were soon crushed by Saddam Hussein's army, the Republican Guard. More than a million Kurdish refugees fled to the borders of Turkey and Iran, but, fearing refugee camps within its borders might foster the Kurdish nationalist movement, Turkey prevented many from entering. About 500,000 Kurdish refugees were forced to remain in northern Iraq, living in makeshift camps in the mountains.

With little food and shelter, thousands of Kurds died. But this time the world was paying attention. As television and newspaper reports told of their plight, some members of the Gulf War coalition took action. France, Great Britain, and the United States established Operation Provide Comfort, an American-led program to provide food and shelter for refugees. The coalition nations also agreed to establish airspace over northern Iraq where Iraqi planes were forbidden to fly. Kurds living in this "no-fly zone," located north of the 36th parallel of latitude, would be protected from future bombing attacks by the Iraqi government.

**Iraqi president Saddam Hussein, holding a rifle, observes a military parade with General Ali Hassan al-Majid. Known to the Kurds as "Chemical Ali," the general was responsible for a number of attacks on Kurdish civilians during the 1980s, including the 1988 massacre at Halabja.**

Within this protected zone, Iraqi Kurds took charge, administering the region as the newly created Kurdish Regional Government (KRG). But although Jalal Talabani's PUK and Massoud Barzani's KDP had united in 1991 to fight against Saddam Hussein, they clashed as rival leaders of the autonomous region. In 1994, an internal war began. Two years into the conflict, the KDP even formed an alliance with Saddam Hussein to fight against the PUK, which was receiving military assistance from Iran. Iraqi troops and tanks initially helped the

KDP defeat its opponents, but the United States stepped in to prevent Saddam from interfering in the region, extending the no-fly zone to within 30 miles (48 km) of Baghdad and striking against Iraqi missile sites in the south.

Bloody warfare between the two major Iraqi Kurdish parties lasted until 1998, when their leaders agreed to officially divide the region between them and signed a peace accord brokered by the United States. But their four-year conflict had caused thousands of deaths and displaced tens of thousands more.

Through the years Saddam continued with his policy of Arabization in Kurdish regions outside the protected zone. In the region of Kirkuk alone, approximately 250,000 Kurds were deported. Those who remained were

**U.S. soldiers carry Kurdish children into a refugee camp, May 1991. When Saddam Hussein attacked Iraq's Kurdish population after losing the Gulf War, hundreds of thousands of Kurds fled from their homes into refugee camps in the mountains along the borders with Turkey and Iran.**

barred from owning property and registering businesses or marriages unless they assumed Arabic names and changed their ethnicity to "Arab" on official documents. Street names and districts received new Arabic names, and Arabs continued to be offered financial rewards for settling in the region.

For years, Iraq disregarded orders by the United Nations that it comply with restrictions imposed after the 1991 Persian Gulf War. U.S.-led forces finally attacked the country in March 2003, which began the second Persian Gulf War. A month later, U.S. troops entered Baghdad, which they took with little resistance. During the combat operations, approximately 70,000 Kurdish militia troops placed themselves under U.S. command and helped take control of the oil-rich towns of Kirkuk and Mosul.

On April 9, 2003, Saddam's regime was officially toppled, and the United States set up a Coalition Provisional Authority (CPA) to administer the war-torn nation until a constitution could be written and elections held. Two months later, the Iraqi Governing Council was appointed, which included Kurds among its members. In March 2004 the Iraqi Governing Council approved a preliminary constitution that allowed for Kurdish representation at the highest level of government.

Violent incidents in Iraq continued after war's end; some of these attacks targeted Kurds because of their support for U.S. intervention in the country. The PUK and KDP suffered a horrific terrorist attack in February 2004 when suicide bombers devastated the two main Kurdish party offices in Arbil. The blasts killed more than 100 Kurds, including the Kurdish deputy prime minister and the city's governor and lieutenant governor. Members of Ansar al-Islam, a group of Kurdish religious extremists who had threatened the PUK and KDP in the past, were blamed for the attacks.

Tensions have remained high between the Kurds and other ethnic groups in northern Iraq as questions over land rights, militias, and the future government have occupied all Iraqi citizens. Some Iraqi Kurds

**Kurdish leader Jalal Talabani signs Iraq's interim constitution during a March 2004 ceremony.**

believe that the autonomous region should break away and form a separate state, while others are willing to be integrated back into Iraq as long as they are permitted some autonomy.

Postwar turmoil, followed by violent clashes and bombings in the cities of Fallujah, Ramadi, and Baghdad in the spring of 2004, threatened the political process in Iraq. The United Nations stepped forward and agreed to help form a central government and set up elections in Iraq. In June the Iraqi Governing Council dissolved itself after a new Iraqi interim government, which includes a Kurdish vice president, was announced.

## A Minority in Iran

In 1921, army officer Reza Khan took power over Iran in a military coup, founding the Pahlavi dynasty and assuming the title of shah.

Although the Kurds in Iran rose up against him in the 1920s, they failed to break away from his government. From 1925 to 1941, the Kurds lived under the rule of Reza Shah Pahlavi, as he was later called. He was succeeded by his son Mohammad Reza Pahlavi.

About 20 years after their first rebellion, Iranian Kurds were briefly successful in creating their own independent nation. In January 1946, Kurdish leader Qazi Mohamed proclaimed the founding of the Mahabad Republic, a new Kurdish nation located in a sliver of northwestern Iraq and based in the town of Mahabad. Qazi Mohamed, who was supported by Iraqi Kurds and the newly created Kurdistan Democratic Party, assumed the presidency. The fledgling nation was backed by the Soviet Union, but vehemently opposed by the Iranian monarchy, Britain, and the United States. When the Soviets abandoned their support, the Mahabad Republic fell within the year to Iranian forces, and its Kurdish founder was hanged.

Several decades later, in the late 1970s, Kurdish nationalists again tried to break away from Iran. The 1979 Islamic revolution that forced Shah Mohammad Reza Pahlavi from power put the country in turmoil. While conservative clerical forces established a Shiite Islamic government headed by religious leader Ayatollah Ruholla Khomeini, Abdul Rahman Qassemlou led the Kurdish Democratic Party of Iran (KDPI) in a bid to gain control of Kurdish land.

From 1979 to 1982, Kurdish guerrilla fighters battled the Islamic Revolution Guards, the Iranian government's armed forces. The Iran-Iraq War began around the same time, and eventually more than 25,000 Kurdish civilians lost their lives in the crossfire. By 1983, the government of the Islamic Republic had regained control of the Kurdish region. It outlawed the KDPI, and those members who had not escaped to northern Iraq were executed. After the Iran-Iraq War ended in 1988, Abdul Rahman Qassemlou and several other well-known Kurdish leaders were assassinated while meeting in Europe with Iranian authorities.

The Islamic Revolution Guards remained in control of the Kurdish areas of Iran until 1998. At that time, Iran's National Security Council declared the region "secure" and transferred responsibility for maintaining law and order to the local police.

Under the shah of Iran the separate Kurdish identity had been recognized, but the government had forbidden Kurds from publishing Kurdish books or speaking their language in public. Many of those involved in Kurdish politics were jailed. Establishment of the new Islamic Republic brought new restrictions, particularly with its enforcement of Islamic law, or *Sharia*, under which strict religious observances became mandatory. Farsi was declared the official language of all Iran, which effectively prevented Kurds from studying in their own language. Nonetheless, Iranian Kurds eventually gained more freedoms than they had enjoyed under the shah.

Beginning in 1998, Iran's president Mohammad Khatami began granting some additional rights to Kurds, allowing them better representation in local governments and opening up cultural opportunities. Some Kurds were elected to Iran's parliament. And with the appropriate government permit in hand, Iranian Kurds could perform traditional plays and music in public. The government also permitted students to learn Kurdish and publishers to produce Kurdish-language newspapers and journals.

However, the Sunni Muslim Kurds are still regarded with some suspicion by the Shiite government because of their religious differences. Iranian leaders also fear that the creation of an independent Kurdistan in Iraq could inspire Kurds in the predominantly Kurdish province of Kordestan to try to break away from Iran.

## A Minority in Syria

Syrian Kurds number approximately 1.5 million in a country of 18 million, or approximately 8 percent of Syria's population. Like Kurds of other

**This rare color image, taken by a Russian photographer around 1905, shows a Kurdish woman with her children.**

countries, Syrian Kurds also struggle for basic rights. For more than 30 years, they lived under emergency law in the Republic of Syria under President Hafiz al-Assad, who upon his death in 2000 was succeeded by his son Bashar.

Although the government initially allowed certain cultural and religious freedoms for Kurds, by the 1950s Syrian laws banned the teaching of Kurdish in schools; the publication of Kurdish-language newspapers, books, or journals; and the formation of Kurdish political parties. In 1961 the government took steps to take lands from Kurds living within the oil-rich al-Jazira region by stripping more than 100,000 of them and their descendants of their citizenship. Two years later, an Arabization resettlement program began forcing many Kurds to move.

Today the number of Kurds in Syria who lack legal citizenship number more than 200,000. They are denied the right to vote, own property, obtain

**Razor wire holds back Kurdish demonstrators outside the Syrian embassy in Nicosia, Cyprus. The Kurds were gathered to protest a series of deadly clashes between Kurds and police in northern Syria that occurred in March 2004.**

government jobs, or even get a passport. Men without citizenship cannot marry Syrian women who are full citizens.

The Kurds of Syria are allowed to speak their native tongue, but they cannot legally publish, teach, or write in Kurdish. At times, Kurdish men have been forbidden from wearing their traditional dress, although there have been no such restrictions on women. Kurds also cannot participate in politics, and activists for reform have been jailed, tortured, exiled, and killed.

The Kurds' frustration over their second-class status has seldom erupted into violence. However, in March 2004 ethnic unrest between Kurds and Arabs at a soccer game in the multi-ethnic city of Qamishli (Kamishli), located north of Damascus, soon developed into antigovernment protests that spread to other cities across northeastern Syria. Demonstrators waved the Kurdish flag, set fire to government buildings, and defaced images and statues of former president Hafiz al-Assad. Government forces fired on the protesters, killing approximately 30 to 40 of them and wounding several hundred more. In the weeks that followed, Syrian police arrested thousands more in crackdowns in the cities of Damascus and Aleppo.

Government officials blamed the Kurdish unrest in Syria on the gains being made by Kurds in Iraq. When the Syrian demonstrations began, authorities noted, Iraqi Kurds had been celebrating the passage of an interim Iraqi constitution that guaranteed Kurds the right to maintain self-rule in Iraq.

A Kurdish man prays in a mosque in Arbil, Iraq. Most of the Kurds follow Islam, the dominant religion of the Middle East, although a small minority practice other religions.

# 4

# The Economy, Politics, and Religion

For centuries Kurds made their living by farming and raising cattle, sheep, and goats; however, with the discovery of oil in the early 20th century and its subsequent development, the means of income have changed for many Kurds.

Centuries ago, farmers from Kurdistan provided much of the region's meat to people living in the surrounding areas of Anatolia, Syria, and Mesopotamia. Today, Kurds still raise livestock for their meat as well as their wool and milk. Sheep and goats are herded to high mountain pastures in the summer, and brought to lowland plains during the winter months. Villagers raise cows and bulls for their meat and milk, and for power in pulling carts and plows. Some Kurds also raise chickens for eggs and meat.

In arable parts of Kurdistan, farmers raise grains (wheat, barley, rye, and oats), as well as crops such as oil seeds (sesame and sunflower), vegetables (tomatoes, cucumber, watermelon, melon, onion, and garlic), fruits (apples, apricots, grapes, olives, peaches, pears, plums, and pomegranates), and legumes (chickpeas, lentils, and green beans). Some fruit and nut trees that grow in the wild in the Zagros and Taurus mountain ranges provide pistachios, almonds, hazelnuts, and chestnuts. The principal cash crops, however, are tobacco and cotton.

In the cities and towns of Turkey, Iraq, Iran, and Syria, many Kurds work as unskilled laborers, particularly in construction. Some do more

**Raising livestock was the way that most Kurds historically made their living. Even today, many Kurds in rural areas care for herds of sheep or goats.**

skilled work as bricklayers, butchers, cattle dealers, and as supervisors or foremen over manual laborers.

Many Kurdish men have spent their lives as fighters, living for years at a time in the rugged mountains of Kurdistan. In the past, Kurdish tribal chiefs supported *peshmerga* fighters, calling them into service when they were needed. More recently, people living in nearby villages have supported *peshmerga* guerrillas with food and other necessities. In Iraq, the term *peshmerga* is also used to refer to those whom political parties hire as militia fighters.

## Manufacturing and Energy

Despite the large amount of cotton and wool that Kurdistan produces and the reputation Kurds have for weaving carpets and *kilims* (richly colored rugs with intricate patterns), the region has no large-scale textile industry. Most cotton and wool is used for local weaving and other Kurdish handicrafts. For the most part, textiles are imported rather than exported.

Mining is a major industry in mineral-rich Kurdistan. Within the Zagros and Taurus ranges lie significant deposits of copper, chromium, iron ore, and coal. Quarries provide construction materials such as granite, limestone, marble, and travertine, as well as raw materials for cement factories.

But more important than mining is petroleum refinement. Rich oil reserves can be found throughout the Kurdish region—around the cities of Rumayla in Syria, Batman and Silvan in Turkey, and Kirkuk and Khaniqin in Iraq. As oil reserves in these regions have been developed, many Kurds have left their rural villages to work as unskilled laborers in the petroleum refineries.

## Poverty and Progress

In theory, Kurdistan's many natural resources—fertile soil, abundant water, and rich mineral reserves—should provide its people with a healthy economy. However, for most of the Kurds' history, other powers have exploited the region's most lucrative resources. As a result, the majority of Kurds in Turkey, Syria, and Iran live in poverty. In most villages, one or two wealthy families own most of the land that is good for farming or for pasturing livestock. The rest of the villagers own either plots just large enough for subsistence farming or no land at all. Landless townspeople usually work as unskilled laborers or as herders for wealthy landowners.

Some Kurdish political groups blame the poverty of the Kurds on the governments of Turkey, Syria, and Iran, claiming they have deliberately chosen not to invest in regions with large Kurdish populations. In all three nations, the public services, infrastructure, education, and health care in Kurdish areas are drastically underdeveloped, especially when compared to areas with predominantly Arab and Turkish populations.

In Turkey, the Kurds' economic situation is also blamed on the years of warfare between the government and the PKK, which has devastated the agricultural economy of the southeastern region. The hundreds of thousands of Kurds displaced by warfare from their villages in Turkey received no foreign aid or government financial assistance. Because of the high poverty rate and massive unemployment in rural areas, many Kurds have moved to cities in search of work.

In Iraq, however, the Kurdish people have fared better than their neighbors. The creation of the no-fly zone over northern Iraq in 1991 promised security and stability, although Iraqi Kurds did not experience economic progress until the late 1990s. Earlier in the decade, they had suffered financial hardships because of the international trade *embargo* imposed on Iraq after the first Persian Gulf War. These economic sanctions were established to punish Iraq for refusing to comply with postwar agreements, which included the disarmament of its weapons program. The economy of Iraqi Kurdistan also struggled because of ongoing warfare between the two major Kurdish factions. Economic growth became attainable only after the KDP and PUK made peace in 1998.

Iraqi Kurdistan also benefited greatly from the United Nations (U.N.) oil-for-food program, instituted in December 1996. The program allowed the Iraqi government in Baghdad to export a limited amount of oil, but the money from oil sales could be used only for the purchase of humanitarian supplies such as food, medicine, and other nonmilitary goods. A portion of the revenue from Iraq's oil sales—13 percent—was allocated specifically for the Kurdish northern region. The Kurds desperately needed the money to rebuild the thousands of villages destroyed by the Baathist government. The stream of Kurdish refugees returning home from Iran to the protection of the no-fly zone also needed housing and food.

U.N. administrators used oil-for-food money to build roads and bridges, houses, schools, health clinics, water and sewerage systems, irrigation networks, and electricity and running water projects in the region. Money from the program and assistance from other small nongovernmental relief organizations (NGOs) also provided medical care such as vaccinations and the distribution of medical supplies to hospitals and clinics. Oil-for-food revenue helped with the massive job of clearing an estimated 12 to 15 million land mines from fields in Iraqi Kurdistan. To ensure that no one went hungry, the U.N. also established a policy that every inhabitant of the north, regardless of income, received a monthly food basket.

Despite the embargo, some diesel fuel and crude oil were illegally smuggled out of Iraq by caravans of trucks traveling through northern Iraq to Turkey. The Kurdistan Democratic Party imposed "tariffs" on oil smugglers at border crossings, and used the revenue to administer the region. Money went for the construction of schools, roads, and hospitals within Kurdistan, and paid the salaries of its militia, local police forces, and teachers.

In addition to the steady revenue from oil, Iraqi Kurdistan attracted private outside investment as well. The region saw a boom in construction projects such as shopping malls, hotel complexes, and an international

**Officials of Iraqi Kurdistan stop a truck to search for contraband at a check-point near Chamchamal, northern Iraq. Revenue collected from truckers illegally smuggling Iraqi oil to Turkey was used to help finance the government of Iraqi Kurdistan.**

airport. By 2002 northern Iraq could boast of bustling cities featuring Internet cafes and shopping bazaars that sold CDs, computers, and cell phones as well as carpets, fruits, and vegetables. According to the Ministry of Reconstruction and Development, between 1992 and 2002 more than half of the 4,000 villages destroyed under Iraq's Baath regime had been rebuilt.

After the 2003 Persian Gulf War, the oil embargo against Iraq was lifted and the oil-for-food program was discontinued, although the Kurds were given former U.N. property such as cars, computers, and power plants as compensation for the program's termination. Around the same time the U.S. Coalition Authority banned oil smuggling and toll and tariff collections at the borders, which had accounted for most of the regional government's revenue. To replace this income, the Kurdistan Regional Government received funding from the U.S.-backed government—enough money to allow the Kurdish government to quadruple the salaries of its employees and militia. However, concerns remained that terrorist attacks in Iraq could damage oil reservoirs, pipelines, or refineries, causing a sudden reduction in oil export revenues.

Although Kurds remain uncertain about how a new central government in Iraq would administer the sharing of the national revenues, authorities in the Kurdistan Regional Government are optimistic about the economic future of their autonomous region.

## Kurdish Politics in Turkey

The violent methods of the Kurdistan Workers Party (PKK), which sought an independent Kurdish state, did not appeal to many Kurds living in Turkey. An outlawed organization, the PKK financed its operations by illegal activities such as the smuggling of drugs and humans. Most Kurds in Turkey preferred to work within the nation's political system to gain recognition of their civil rights. But such efforts were often difficult. Turkish authorities jailed many Kurdish teachers and politicians for advocating for the right to speak and teach in their native tongue.

During the 1990s four pro-Kurdish political parties, all calling for laws that guaranteed equal rights for Kurds, were banned in succession. In 1991, several Kurdish deputies (officials elected to Turkey's National Assembly) formed the People's Labor Party (Halkin Emek Partisi, or HEP); within two years, Turkey's Constitutional Court had declared the fledgling party illegal. The deputies then formed a new political party with similar goals, called the Democracy Party (Demokrasi Partisi, or DEP). By 1994, DEP was banned, and several of its supporters jailed. Next came the

People's Democratic Party (Halkin Demokrasi Partisi, or HADEP), which, after it was banned in 1999, changed its name to the Democratic People's Party, or DEHAP. Today, it is considered the civilian voice of Kurdish nationalism in Turkey.

According to some accounts, DEHAP is still facing opposition from the government. Representatives of DEHAP reported in 2003 that its members were being imprisoned for various charges. However, there have been some political victories, as several DEHAP members won mayoral offices in various southeastern towns during 2003 elections.

Over the years a number of Kurds have been leaders in the Turkish government, holding high positions as foreign ministers or even prime ministers. However, those who scaled the ranks in Turkish government and society often did so because they deliberately did not identify themselves as Kurds. In fact, many Kurds, especially those who live in the western cities or who have married Turks, do not consider ethnic identity in politics and do not vote exclusively for the Kurdish party.

Although the Kurdish Congress for Freedom and Democracy (KADEK)—the new name of the PKK—has stated that its sole aim is to ensure Kurds their cultural, linguistic, and general human rights, the Turkish government continued to consider KADEK an illegal political party. In November 2003 KADEK was disbanded and replaced by the

**The most widely used version of the Kurdish flag consists of a yellow sun placed between bands of red, white, and green. The golden sun disk, an ancient Kurdish symbol, emblazons the center. From the time of the Ottoman Empire, Kurdish groups have raised this flag in defiance against oppressive rule.**

A Kurd casts his vote in Turkey's November 2002 parliamentary election at a polling station in the southeastern city of Diyarbakir. Most Kurds living in Turkey reject the violent methods of the PKK and other radical groups. They prefer instead to improve their situation through peaceful means such as voting.

Kurdistan People's Congress (KONGRA-GEL), which was also quickly labeled by Turkey and several world nations as a terrorist organization.

## Kurdish Politics in Iraq

Iraq's autonomous Kurdish region consists of the three northern *governorates* (provinces) of Iraq: Arbil, Dahuk, and as-Sulaymaniyah. In May 1992, the Kurds living there elected a joint 105-member representative regional assembly, a parliament that met in the city of Arbil. This assembly consisted of 50 members from each of the two major parties (the KDP and PUK), and in an effort to establish equal rights for minorities (including the Turkmen, Assyrians, Chaldeans, and Arabs), the assembly also included five representatives from minority parties.

The new government announced the creation of a Kurdish state administered by the Kurdish Regional Government (KRG) that ultimately had two administrations, two prime ministers, and two militia. The KDP government, headed by Massoud Barzani and based in the city of Arbil, controlled the rural northwestern regions, while the PUK government, led by Jalal Talabani, administered the more urban southeastern lands from its base in as-Sulaymaniyah.

Although friction between the two major parties resulted in civil war from 1994 to 1998, by 2002 Iraqi Kurdistan had made great gains and could boast of many features similar to that of an independent nation: it had three universities, more than 50 newspapers and magazines, two satellite television stations and numerous radio stations, and a Kurdish school curriculum, not to mention its own Kurdish army and flag. Because the region was still part of Iraq, its government used Iraqi passports (that the KRG government processed) and currency (Iraqi dinars that the KRG had printed in Switzerland).

In June 2003, after the second Gulf War was declared over, the two separate KDP and PUK governments agreed to create a unified Kurdish government. The KDP prime minister, Nechirvan Barzani, Massoud's nephew, became the KRG prime minister. Both Massoud Barzani and Talabani, along with three other Kurds, were appointed to the 25-member Iraqi Governing Council set up by the U.S.-run Coalition Provisional Authority. The coalition government also included five ministries run by Kurds, including water and foreign affairs.

Although other Iraqi militias were banned after the end to hostilities was declared, the KDP and PUK were allowed to keep their *peshmerga* armies, intelligence forces, and prisons. (Kurdish militiamen now wear the Iraqi army uniform, but many feature a Kurdish flag patch on the shoulder.) However, the separate Kurdish currency was abolished as of January 2004, having been replaced by the new Iraqi dinar in October 2003.

In March 2004, the Iraqi Governing Council officially approved the interim Iraqi constitution. The preliminary constitution established the

Presidency Council, consisting of a president and two deputy presidents. To attain equal representation, these three positions had to be filled by one Shiite Arab, one Sunni Arab, and one Sunni Kurd. In turn, the Presidency Council would appoint a prime minister, members of a council of ministers, and a nine-member federal Supreme Court for Iraq.

The interim constitution allowed minority groups such as Kurds and Sunni Arabs to veto the permanent constitution. In other words, they have the right to object to any law—a provision that was opposed by the majority Shiite leaders. The document also affirmed that the Iraqi Kurds would keep their regional government, elected assembly, and police. Kurdish was also listed as an official language of Iraq.

**This photo shows the exterior of the parliament building of Iraqi Kurdistan in Arbil. With the U.S. no-fly zone preventing Saddam Hussein from attacking Iraqi Kurdistan between 1992 and 2003, the Kurds were able to create a de facto autonomous state in northern Iraq.**

Planning began for the election of a 275-member transitional National Assembly of Iraq. This body would also be responsible for drafting a permanent constitution that would be voted upon in a nationwide referendum scheduled for 2005. Local elections in Iraqi Kurdistan would be held at the same time.

In June 2004 the Iraqi Governing Council was dissolved and a new Iraqi interim government was installed according to the terms of the interim constitution. Representing the Kurds in the new government were Vice President Rowsch Shaways from the KDP and Iraqi Deputy Prime Minister for National Security Barham Saleh, a former PUK prime minister.

## Kurdish Politics in Iran and Syria

Iran is an Islamic republic with a Shiite majority. Among the armed political groups opposing the government is the Democratic Party of Iranian Kurdistan (KDPI), a nationalist movement that has been pushed into northern Iraq. This is territory controlled by Iraq's PUK, which has received support in the past from the Iranian government. Although both the PUK and KDPI are Kurdish groups, the PUK has remained separate from the KDPI and has even prevented it from using Iraq as a base to launch attacks on Iran.

In general, Iranian Kurds can participate in politics; some have even become members of parliament. However, before the spring 2004 elections the Iranian government disqualified candidates who were pushing for reforms, and many of them were Kurds. More conservative hardliners came into power, and they currently dominate the Iranian parliament. Some analysts believe this crackdown occurred because of government concerns over the large public celebrations in Iran that accompanied the March 2004 approval of Iraq's interim constitution, a document that essentially granted autonomy to Iraqi Kurds.

Although Kurds in Syria cannot legally form political parties, some operate within the one-party system of the National Progressive Front (NPF). Some Kurds have attained membership in parliament, but have limited powers. The Kurdish Leadership Console in Western Kurdistan (KLC) is a group that represents major Kurdish groups and tribal leaders working to achieve cultural and political rights for Syrian Kurds.

## Religion

Most Kurds (about 75 to 85 percent) are Sunni Muslims, which is also the majority faith in Turkey. As many as 15 percent of Kurds belong to the Shia sect of Islam, the predominant faith in Iraq and Iran. Most Shiite Kurds live in Iran, where they make up about one-third of the Iranian Kurdish population.

The Islamic faith dictates much of the way of life for its followers by establishing a specific code of behavior, ethics, and habits. Among the practices of the devout Muslim is praying five times a day while facing Mecca, the birthplace of the religion's founder, the prophet Muhammad.

A majority of Kurds also participate in one of many mystical Islamic sects called Sufi orders, or *tariqa*. Major Sufi orders include the Bektashi in northwest Kurdistan, Naqshbandi in western and northern Kurdistan, Kadiri in eastern and central Kurdistan, and Nurbakhshi in southern Kurdistan. The holy men of different *tariqa* orders are called *sheikhs* (also spelled *shaykhs*). Sufi practices involve many non-Islamic rites and rituals, such as meditation, trances, ecstatic utterances, and self-mutilation (such

A small number of Kurds who follow the Jewish faith once lived in southern regions of Kurdistan; they migrated to Israel during the 1950s.

**A Kurdish man prays on the roof of the historic temple of Yezidis in the village of Lalesh, Iraq. There are about 300,000 Yezidis worldwide, most of whom are Kurds who live in northern Iraq, Iran, Turkey, Syria, the former Soviet Union, and western Europe (particularly Germany).**

as piercing the skin with daggers or skewers). Such mystical practices are performed to attain communion with God, but they often offend strictly orthodox Muslims.

A minority of Kurds are neither Sunni nor Shia Muslims. A few follow the Christian faith. The rest belong to one of three religions referred to as the Cult of Angels because their followers believe in the existence of seven divine angels as well as one God. Two Cult of Angels religions draw upon the principles of the Shia Islam: the Alevis (1.5 million Kurds), who live mostly in eastern Turkey, and the Ahl-e Haqq (about 700,000 Kurds), who reside mostly near the Iran-Iraq border. Turks, Arabs, and other ethnic groups besides Kurds practice the Alevi Muslim and Ahl-e Haqq faiths.

The small faction of believers in Yezidism, the third faith in the Cult of Angels, is made up exclusively of Kurds. Yezidism has been referred to as the original Kurdish religion because of its ancient origins. The religion combines pre-Islamic beliefs adopted from Zoroastrianism (a Persian religion founded between 1000 and 700 B.C.) as well as aspects of Christianity, Judaism, and Sufism. Yezidis pray three times a day, while facing the sun. Numbering about 300,000, they live mostly in northern Iraq.

A Kurdish woman, wearing a traditional garment called an *abaya*, walks down the steps of a carpet shop in Arbil, Iraq. The Kurds have a reputation for weaving intricate patterns into richly colored rugs called *kilims*.

# 5

## The People

$S$ince the 1960s the numbers of Kurds in the Middle East have been steadily growing, and today they represent about 15 percent of the region's population. However, because the nations in which Kurds live often do not identify them as a separate ethnic group in census surveys, reliable statistical information is hard to come by.

### The Tribal Identity

Before the 1980s, Kurdish society was mainly rural and people lived in small villages scattered over the mountainsides. However, groups of villages remained connected with one other because their inhabitants belonged to the same tribe and followed the same leader. Tribes are groups of several families whose many members share a common ancestor and ownership of lands. Kurdish tribes established claim to certain lands, or the rights to use pasturelands owned by other tribes.

Ultimate control of territory traditionally lay with the tribal leader to whom Kurds gave absolute loyalty. In the past, this tribal chief, or *agha*, had absolute power, although today he serves mostly as a representative and advisor for his people. The tribal leader settles disputes, allocates land and water use, and maintains order over the villages within his jurisdiction, often with the aid of a council. Villages pay taxes to the *agha* in the form of cash or produce. Kurdish lands also may be controlled by religious leaders, or *sheikhs*, who serve the role of tribal chiefs. Individual villages are led by the *mukhtar,* or village chief.

Some Kurdish tribes are actually coalitions—groups of people of different ancestry who have banded together to form an entire tribe. Loyalty to the tribe and its chief is of utmost important to traditional, rural Kurds, although groups may change their allegiances. In many cases, tribes form their own regional political groups. Although the *agha* is not as powerful as he was in the past, many Kurds prefer to give him their trust and obedience rather than deal with state authorities.

Tribal identity is not as important to Kurds living in villages and cities, particularly those who have assimilated into non-Kurdish cities such as Istanbul and Tehran. However, many rural Kurds consider loyalty to their particular tribe and tribal leader of the highest importance.

## *Language and Literature*

The Kurdish language differs markedly from Turkish and Arabic. As an Indo-European language similar to Persian, it is closer to English, French, and German. Kurdish exists in many different dialects. There are two main dialects that the majority of Kurds speak: Kermanji (also called Northern Kurdish or Kurmanci) and Sorani (Southern Kurdish). Kermanji is spoken by Kurds living in Turkey, in far northern Iraq (north of the Greater Zab River), and in parts of northern Iran, Syria, Armenia, and

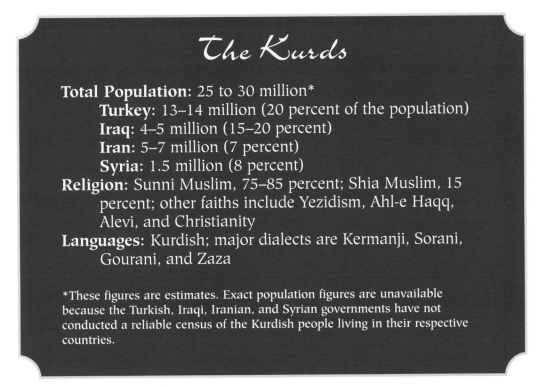

## The Kurds

**Total Population:** 25 to 30 million*
  **Turkey:** 13–14 million (20 percent of the population)
  **Iraq:** 4–5 million (15–20 percent)
  **Iran:** 5–7 million (7 percent)
  **Syria:** 1.5 million (8 percent)
**Religion:** Sunni Muslim, 75–85 percent; Shia Muslim, 15 percent; other faiths include Yezidism, Ahl-e Haqq, Alevi, and Christianity
**Languages:** Kurdish; major dialects are Kermanji, Sorani, Gourani, and Zaza

*These figures are estimates. Exact population figures are unavailable because the Turkish, Iraqi, Iranian, and Syrian governments have not conducted a reliable census of the Kurdish people living in their respective countries.

Georgia. Sorani is spoken by Iraqi Kurds living south of the Greater Zab and in much of Iran.

Other dialects include Zaza, spoken by Kurds living in northeastern Turkey and parts of northern Iran; and Gourani, spoken in parts of southern Iran. Speakers of northern and southern Kermanji can usually understand one another, but some Kurdish dialects differ so much their speakers cannot effectively communicate. More educated Kurds are usually bilingual, and in addition to Kurdish speak Turkish in Turkey, Farsi in Iran, or Arabic in Iraq or Syria.

Both Zaza and Gourani are spoken dialects only, while the Kermanji and Sorani dialects are written as well as spoken. The alphabet used to write in Kurdish differs by country: in Turkey, the Latin alphabet is used; in the former Soviet Union, it is the Cyrillic alphabet; and in Iraq and Syria, Kurdish writings are in a modified form of Arabic. Thus, Kermanji is usually written in Latin script, while Sorani is written in modified Arabic script.

The first written history of the Kurdish people, called *Sharafnama*, was penned by Prince Sharaf al-Din Bitlisi in 1597. The book, whose title means "book of princes," describes the histories of the various Kurdish tribes. The author, born in a ruling family in northern Kurdistan, detailed many aspects of the Kurdish culture as well as the impact that different empires had on the people.

Kurdish literature largely consists of epic poems and tales of folklore, and many of them deal with heroism, romance, and the love of country. The poet Ahmad Khani (1651–1707) is said to have inspired Kurdish nationalism in 1695 with his epic *Mem o Zin*. This 17th-century poem tells of the doomed love between two young people of different tribes: a boy named Mem and girl named Zin who is already betrothed to another. Along with being a romantic tale, the poem celebrates Kurdish culture, discusses the Kurds' place among nations, and indicates a desire for self-governance that existed even then. The following excerpt from *Mem o Zin* reflects the poet's sentiment that Kurdish oppression will end:

> Look! Our misfortune has reached its zenith,
> Has it started to come down do you think?
> Or will it remain so,
> Until comes upon us the end of time?
> Is it possible, I wonder, that for us too,
> A star will emerge out of the firmament?
> Let luck be on our side for once.

Kurdish-language publications were prohibited by the Ottoman empire. To circumvent this ban, the first Kurdish-language newspaper was published outside Kurdistan—in Cairo, Egypt, in 1898. Because Syria and Turkey, where the Kermanji dialect is spoken, outlawed Kurdish-language publications for so many years, much modern Kurdish literature has been written in Sorani. In fact, during the 20th century more than 80 percent of all Kurdish books published were written in Sorani.

## Education

Kurds living in Iraq have had the best opportunities to learn the Kurdish language in government-run schools, but only since the establishment of self-government in 1992. Early in Saddam Hussein's rule, the Iraqi government made some concessions to Kurdish demands and permitted the founding of the School for Kurdish Studies at Baghdad University and the establishment of a Kurdish branch at the University of Sulaymaniyah. However, children in the government-run schools were educated only in Arabic.

**A Kurdish student at the University of Sulaymaniyah uses a computer. Students in Iraqi Kurdistan have been able to take classes in their native language since 1992.**

After 1992, when an autonomous regional government assumed control over Iraqi Kurdistan, children under 10 were no longer taught in Arabic, but in Kurdish instead. Although some Kurds point with pride to this achievement, others remain concerned that this younger Kurdish-educated generation may have problems in the future because they will be unfamiliar with the Arabic that their neighbors speak.

Turkey has allowed Kurdish-language schools since 2003, but the legislation applies only to private schools. The language is not taught in the government-supported public schools. Today, only a small number of Kurds in Turkey can read and write in Kurdish because the language was outlawed for so long.

Some private schools and universities in Iran offer courses on the Kurdish culture and language; however, the language is not taught in the schools. Syria does not allow Kurdish to be spoken in any public gatherings, including schools.

## Marriage and Family Life

In strictly traditional Kurdish households, it is understood that Kurds must marry Kurds, and it is not unusual for extended family members such as cousins to wed. As is common in other parts of the Middle East, parents usually arrange marriages. In some cases, men who have gone abroad for study or work will come back home when it is time to marry and select from the prospects chosen by their mothers.

For traditional Kurds, arranged marriages involve an elaborate negotiation process. After the woman agrees to marry the man, his family makes a formal request. Then both families discuss the conditions and bride-price, which is paid by the groom's family as gold, money, or property. In Kurdish society, gold and silver jewelry is a sign of wealth. The groom's family hosts the wedding, which can last two or three days and include hundreds of guests.

In accordance with Islamic law, men are expected to marry, and husbands may have more than one wife, particularly if the first marriage has not produced a son. In the past, large families with more than 10 children were typical in many Kurdish homes, and their extended families often numbered in the hundreds. Today, the typical family has three or four children.

In the strictly orthodox, or traditional, Muslim world, men and women must adhere to strict Islamic laws governing behavior and dress. For example, one of the tenets of Islam is showing proper hospitality. Visitors in a Kurdish household are warmly greeted with handshakes and offered candy, tea, and fruit. Kurds indicate their willingness to help someone by placing the hands over the eyes, and saying the common Kurdish expression *Ser chaow*, which literally means "on my eyes." This gesture and phrase simply mean "at your service."

**Members of a Kurdish family celebrate a wedding.**

> For centuries, Kurds traditionally did not have last names, or surnames. They adopted last names only during the 20th century, when forced to do so by the governments of the nations in which they lived. Many Kurds followed the Arab tradition of taking their father's name as the middle name and the name of their tribe or region as the last name. Others took a grandfather's or great-grandfather's first name as their new surname.

Kurds tend to be more moderate than orthodox Muslims in their interpretations of Islamic law regarding acceptable behavior and dress for women. Kurdish women usually do not cover their faces or wear the *abaya* (or *chador*)—a long, black garment that orthodox Muslim women wear to completely cover the body. In most parts of Kurdistan, women can work outside the home: rural Kurdish women work in the fields, while many urban dwellers attend classes at schools and universities or work in businesses.

However, in more conservative parts of Iraqi Kurdistan, women are largely relegated to maintaining responsibility for the home. Most do not go out after 5:00 P.M. unless accompanied by their families; in Iraq's conservative cities women often do not go out by themselves at all. In rural parts of Kurdistan most women do not drive, travel by themselves, or spend the night away from home unless they are with male relatives. One's behavior reflects on the family, so most women feel bound to follow the dictates of the Kurdish society in which they live.

## Traditional Dress and Customs

Traditional Kurdish clothes are colorful, sparkling with sequins and glittering gold and silver threads woven into bright fabrics. Patterns and colors vary according to the region and usually identify the wearer's tribe or political party. For example, the color of Iraq's PUK political party is yellow, while green identifies members of the KDP. Men of the Barzan region commonly sport turbans of red and white.

Kurdish men wear baggy trousers with a shirt and a short jacket, or *shalwar*. Together the trousers and jacket are called *shal u shapik*. An elaborately woven cummerbund (waistband) or decorative sash adorns the waist, and a skullcap and square of fabric tightly tied as a turban covers the head. The military-style *shal u shapik* is also known as *khak*.

The traditional dress for women also consists of loose trousers, but these are covered by a long, loose-fitting dress or caftan. To keep themselves warm, Kurdish women may wear several layers of dresses. A short vest often completes the outfit. Women also cover their head with a headscarf called a *sarbend*. In Turkey the women's headscarves are often edged with lace.

Kurdish everyday dress differs from one region to the next. Women in urban areas of Iran typically wear the *abaya* or *chador* on the city streets because it is required by the Islamic government. In Iraq, more traditional Kurdish women also wear the *abaya*, although the garment is seldom seen in Turkey. More conservative Kurdish women in Iran and Iraq cover their faces with a garment called a *kheli* whenever they are in public. At home many Kurdish women wear whatever they wish.

Some Kurds today follow Western fashion, and their clothing can range from knee- or calf-length skirts and blouses for women or a three-piece suit for men to T-shirts and jeans for both. Many young people wear the tradi-

It was not until September 2003 that the Turkish law forbidding Kurds from giving their children Kurdish names was lifted. However, parents still cannot use any names that contain the letters q, x, and w, which are found in the Kurdish alphabet but not in the Turkish one.

**A group of Kurdish girls wear brightly colored traditional garments while walking to a picnic in the countryside of northern Iraq.**

tional dress only for special occasions, while it is everyday attire for older generations. In Iran many Kurdish men typically wear Western clothes in public, but feel more comfortable in baggy Kurdish trousers at home.

A traditional piece of Kurdish jewelry is the *parang*. This style of jewelry, no longer in fashion, consists of many gold and silver coins on a chain that is worn around the neck or waist or along the brim of a hat or turban.

## Music

The poetry of the Kurds often appears in their songs, and there are songs for every occasion. Some are featured only at special occasions, such as wedding or holiday celebrations. Others have religious ties; for example, some *gouranis* are sung in villages and cities during the Islamic month of **Ramadan** to herald the coming of dawn (when Muslims can have food before they begin their fast for the day). A funeral procession might be accompanied by the singing of *chemari gouranis,* sad songs that usually lament the loss of a young person.

Music is not just for special occasions, it is a part of everyday life. There are Kurdish lullabies, children's songs, and work songs. For instance, rural women working in the fields may sing traditional songs as they go about their chores of milking the cows or carrying water from the springs. Although the broadcast of Kurdish songs on television or the radio was banned for many years in Iraq, Iran, and Turkey, the music lived on, eventually making its way to Kurdistan via satellite television networks.

Singing is often accompanied by stringed instruments such as lutes (regional variations of the instrument include the *saz, tambur,* and *oud*); percussion instruments (*dehol,* a large cylindrical drum); and wind instruments such as oboes (*zurna, nerme ney, balaban*) and flutes (*shimshal* or *dudik*).

Playing instruments, singing songs, and line dancing enliven picnics, which are a common tradition in Kurdistan. Such events include setting up tents, building bonfires for barbecues, and sharing in the company of friends and family members while enjoying good food and drink.

## Cuisine

The Kurdish diet consists mostly of vegetables and grains, although the Kurds eat lamb, mutton, and chicken as well as some beef. They prefer meat that has been butchered according to Islamic law so that it is *halal,* or pure. Islamic dietary laws forbid the consumption of pork, although wild pigs and boars are common in Kurdistan.

Meats are usually cooked in dishes with rice or bulgur (a kind of wheat) and vegetables, or they are simmered in rich stews. Among popular Kurdish dishes are *biryani* rice, made with raisins, nuts, and chicken; *tershick*, wheat patties filled with vegetables and lamb; and *dughabba*, wheat patties stuffed with ground lamb and served in a mint-flavored goat's milk broth.

Meals commonly include vegetables such as eggplant, summer squash, cucumbers, and tomatoes that have been flavored with salt, pepper, cumin, garlic, and cooking oil. Pomegranate juice is also a common ingredient in many Kurdish dishes. Fruits such as apricots, watermelon, and fresh or dried grapes may be offered to visiting guests as a snack or part of a meal.

**Members of an extended Kurdish family eat dinner together at a home in Qamishli, Syria.**

An essential part of a Kurdish breakfast is *nan tanik* (a large doughy flat bread that has been baked on a circular iron mound heated by coals). It is usually served with local white cheese that is made from curdled milk and flavored with herbs. It may be eaten with plain yogurt, honey, and tea.

A typical Middle Eastern drink, called *du*, consists of yogurt and water. Kurds commonly drink *chai*, a strongly sugared tea usually served in small, tulip-shaped glasses. Most Iranian Kurds drink *chai* Persian-style: with a sugar cube held in the mouth.

## Kurdish Festivals

The biggest festival for the Kurds, no matter what nation they live in, is Newroz, which means "new dawn" in Kurdish. For the Kurds, the first day of spring is the first day of the year, so the holiday is also referred to as the Kurdish New Year. Newroz falls during the **vernal equinox**— around March 20th or 21st. Some believe the holiday had its origins in the Zoroastrian faith, an ancient religion more than 2,700 years old.

For the Kurds, the story behind Newroz is one of victory over tyranny. According to one Kurdish legend, a tyrannical Persian king named Rustom ruled over the Kurds about 2,500 years ago. One day, a young Kurdish ironsmith called Kawa decided to end Rustom's rule. He told his fellow Kurds that he would light a fire on the highest mountain peak as a signal that it was time for them all to attack the palace. The plan worked. The Kurds stormed the king's fortress, allowing Kawa to kill the ruthless dictator. Other versions of the story explain that news of the king's overthrow was spread to the rest of Kurdistan by people lighting signal fires, sending the word from mountaintop to mountaintop.

Kurds today celebrate the tyrant's defeat by lighting small bonfires in the streets and hills and jumping over them. Some believe the ritual of jumping over the flames cleanses them of impurities. During Newroz, families gather for picnics or visit with family and friends, sometimes exchanging small gifts.

**Waving a red, gold, and green rope (the colors of the Kurdish flag), a woman dances with her husband inside a circle, with friends and neighbors clapping, at the annual Newroz celebration near the city of Diyarbakir in southeastern Turkey. Newroz celebrates the first day of spring and the first day of the Kurdish new year.**

Newroz is a national holiday for all citizens of Iran, but it is a major holiday to the Kurds, who see it as a celebration of their nationality and culture. In Iraq's Kurdistan Region Newroz is an official three-day holiday. In Turkey the holiday has often been banned because the bonfire celebrations have led to violence between government authorities and ethnic Kurds.

As Muslims, Kurds also observe the major Islamic holidays. One of the most important is the Feast of the Sacrifice, or Eid al-Adha (also called Eid al-Qurban). This day celebrates the story told in the Qur'an of the patriarch Abraham's willingness to sacrifice his son Ishmael to Allah. Because Abraham obeyed God, the boy was spared and a ram was sacrificed in his place. Kurds celebrate Eid al-Adha with a ritual slaughter of a sheep or goat. Over a four-day-long festival, family and community members gather and feast together, and donate a portion of the meal to the poor.

A second feast, Eid al-Fitr, celebrates the end of Ramadan, the ninth month of the Islamic lunar calendar. During the month of Ramadan, adult Muslims refrain from eating and drinking during daylight hours. By fasting, they practice self-control and work to become more spiritual in their faith. They also develop a better compassion for those who are poor and must fast because they have no food. At sundown, faithful Muslims break their fast. At the end of Ramadan, they hold the major feast of Eid-al-Fitr to mark the end of the period of self-sacrifice.

A view of Istanbul, the largest city in Turkey. More Kurds live in Istanbul than in any other city in the world.

# 6

# Cities and Communities

*M*ost Kurds today live in cities and villages instead of on farms. Forced evictions, warfare, and extreme poverty have pushed many rural Kurds to urban areas.

## Major Kurdish Cities in Turkey

In Turkey, some Kurdish migrants moved to western cities with majority Turkish populations, such as Ankara and Istanbul. Others settled in large cities in southeastern Turkey, a region that has 10 Turkish provinces with majority Kurd populations. Many poor and homeless Kurds found shelter in shantytowns called *gecekondus* that sprang up on the edges of both Turkish and Kurdish cities.

The predominantly Turkish city of Istanbul has attracted Kurdish migrants for centuries. Approximately 2 million Kurds live in the city today, a much-larger Kurdish population than that of Diyarbakir, which is Turkey's largest city with majority Kurdish population.

Diyarbakir is the capital of the Turkish province bearing the same name. More than 600,000 inhabitants live in this major urban center, the ninth largest in Turkey. Located in southeastern Turkey atop a plateau next to the Tigris River, the city was founded around 1500 B.C. It subsequently was ruled by Arabs, Seljuk Turks, and Persians before being conquered by the Ottoman Turks in 1515. During the 1990s and early 2000, more than 300,000 displaced Kurdish villagers fled to *gecekondus* that grew up around Diyarbakir, swelling its population to almost a million.

An ancient town, Diyarbakir contains many mosques and churches. The city features one of the oldest mosques in Turkey—the 11th century Ulu Mosque. Among the city's most striking landmarks are the black basalt ruins of fortress walls that encircle the town and date from the fourth century A.D.

This Kurdish city is a trade center for agricultural crops such as grains, melons, and cotton, as well as for mineral products such as copper ore and petroleum—all of which are produced in the surrounding region. Major manufactures include flour, wine, textiles, and machinery. Diyarbakir also has an international airport and a major university.

Archeologists have found evidence that the city of Erzurum, located in eastern Turkey, existed during the fifth century A.D. Then called Theodosiopolis, it served as an important fortress for the Byzantine empire. The city is celebrated by Turks as the site of the first national Turkish Congress, headed by Mustafa Kemal Atatürk in 1919.

Modern Erzurum claims a population of almost 400,000, which makes it the 16th-largest city in Turkey and the country's second-largest Kurdish city. It serves as a major agricultural trade center for crops grown in the region, such as sugar beets, wheat, barley, and vegetables. Erzurum is also known for its metal and leather handicrafts, and is an important railroad center.

Located in eastern Turkey, Van sits along the edge of the country's largest lake, also called Van. The city dates to the 13th century B.C. when it was founded as the capital of the kingdom of Urartu, or Ararat. During World War I, the town and surrounding region saw bitter fighting, as Turkish and Kurdish forces battled Armenians and Russians. Ultimately the original city of Van was destroyed by the Ottomans, after which it was captured by the Russians in 1915. Following the creation of the Turkish Republic in 1923, the government erected a new city of Van a few miles east of the original town.

Today Van is a predominantly Kurdish city that serves as a market center for local Kurdish farmers selling fruits and grains. Its population of more than 300,000 makes it the country's third-largest Kurdish city.

## Major Kurdish Cities in Iraq

The three largest cities within Iraqi Kurdistan have the same names as the governorates in which they are located: Arbil, as-Sulaymaniyah, and Dahuk. However, two other important cities of Iraq that the Kurds count as

**Erzurum, a city in eastern Turkey, was once an important stopping point on the trade routes that connected Asia and Europe. Today, it has a large Kurdish population.**

their own, but that also contain large numbers of other ethnic groups, are Mosul and Kirkuk.

Arbil (known as Hawler in Kurdish) is located in the southern part of the Kurdish autonomous region. It hosts a mostly Kurdish population of almost 900,000 residents. The fourth-largest city in Iraq, Arbil is the country's largest predominantly Kurdish city.

One of the world's oldest continuously inhabited towns, Arbil was founded before 2300 B.C. as the ancient Sumerian city of Urbilum. Later it served as an important trading center because of its strategic location along the caravan route between the cities of Baghdad and Mosul. Today, the city hosts the headquarters of the KDP and is the seat of the Kurdish parliament. It is also a major commercial and agricultural center.

**Kurds walk through a market in Arbil, the largest Kurdish city in Iraq.**

During the 1990s, Arbil was devastated as the PUK and KDP fought for power in northern Iraq. Since 2000, the city has seen significant rebuilding as well as new construction. It now features a Kurdish studies academy, the Iraq Institute of Democracy, Salahaddin University, and parks with amphitheaters for musical performances. The newly constructed Hawler International Airport opened in June 2003.

The sixth-largest city in Iraq and the nation's second-largest Kurdish city, as-Sulaymaniyah is home to more than 680,000 residents. It is a relatively young city, compared with many of its neighbors, having been founded around 1785 by the Baban princes (one of the most influential Kurdish dynasties), who made it the capital of their emirate. In 1919, Sheikh Mahmoud Barzinji led the first of many uprisings against the British here, and in 1923 declared it part of his newly formed kingdom of Kurdistan. British bombs forced him out of the city, but he continued to fight from the mountains until 1927.

As-Sulaymaniyah lies in northeastern Iraq, near the border with Iran. It has been under the jurisdiction of the PUK since 1991, and refugee camps on the city's outskirts have served as a safe haven for many displaced Kurds.

The first Kurdish press was established in as-Sulaymaniyah in 1920, and the city has since remained a center for Kurdish publishing. Today, with its numerous offices and hotels, as-Sulaymaniyah serves as an important trade and administrative center for the Kurdish autonomous region. The first Kurdish school of higher education, the University of Sulaymaniyah, was founded here in 1968.

The major urban center of Dahuk serves the provinces along the Turkish border. Traditionally under the jurisdiction of the KDP, Dahuk has a predominantly Kurdish population of approximately 400,000. In downtown Dahuk stands the Institute of Fine Arts and the University of Dahuk, both founded in 1992, after the area fell under the protection of the no-fly zone.

Located in the Ninawa governorate, Mosul has a population of approximately 1.8 million, making it the largest city of Iraqi Kurdistan and one of the largest cities in Iraq.

Because of its strategic location on the Tigris River, Mosul was an important commercial trade center of the region from the 8th to the 13th centuries. It was particularly known for its fine-quality cotton goods, called muslin, a fabric named for the city. Mosul was also renowned for its fine marble.

The discovery and subsequent development of oil reserves in the region surrounding Mosul have made the province immensely valuable. The region was occupied by the British following World War I, and soon afterward became part of the British mandate of Iraq. The Kurdish people continue to claim the land for their own, as does the Turkish Republic and the people in southern Iraq.

Mosul's population is mostly Arab, although the surrounding region is inhabited mainly by Kurds. The city lost much of its Kurdish population during the 1970s and 1980s through Saddam Hussein's Arabization program, when Kurds were forced from the region, although many have since returned.

Mosul serves as an agricultural trade center for regional crops and livestock. It is also a manufacturing center for oil, cement, and textiles. Railroads link the city to major cities within Iraq, while roads connect the city with Turkey. Mosul is also home to Mosul University.

Located about 90 miles (145 km) south of Mosul, Kirkuk lies within the at-Ta'mim governorate of Iraq. With a population of more than 780,000, Kirkuk is Iraq's fifth-largest city.

In 1934, development of Kirkuk's oil field began, and the city quickly became an important center of the petroleum industry. Two parallel oil pipelines, built in 1977 and 1987, carry oil from Kirkuk to the port city of Ceyhan, Turkey, on the Mediterranean Sea. The region in and around the

Famed explorer Marco Polo (1254–1324) mentioned the present-day towns of Mosul, Iraq, and Mush and Mardin in Turkey in a journal of his travels along the Silk Road, the major trading route between China and Europe. According to his notes, long ago the residents of these towns were "manufacturers and traders," famous for their cotton fabrics.

city is Iraq's largest oil producer. Oil analysts estimate that Kirkuk has reserves of approximately 8.7 billion barrels, or as much as 40 percent of the oil reserves of Iraq. Besides serving as a major oil producer, Kirkuk is also a trade center for the region's agriculture, with major crops such as cereals, olives, fruits, and cotton. The city is also home to some textile manufacturing.

The Kurds consider Kirkuk their economic and cultural center, and those who propose an independent Kurdish state would like to see it as the capital. However, the city is located outside the Kurdish autonomous region, just to its south, and Arabs, Assyrian Christians, and Turkmen (an ethnic group related to the Turks) also claim the city as their own.

Much of Kirkuk's heavily Kurdish and Turkomen ethnic population changed during the 1970s and 1980s because of Saddam Hussein's Arabization programs. During the 2003 Persian Gulf War in Iraq, Kurdish forces captured the city. This power shift resulted in a mass migration of Arabs from Kirkuk, as well as a return of its Kurdish population. However, ethnic tensions and riots between Arabs, Turkomen, and Kurds continue to devastate the city.

Following the 2003 Gulf War, Kurdish leaders continued to keep a strong presence in Kirkuk. In June 2003, the Shafaq cultural center, which celebrates the Kurdish language and culture, opened in the city.

# Major Kurdish Cities in Iran and Syria

Most Iranian Kurds live in the western part of the country, in the midst of the Zagros mountain range that runs parallel to the borders of Turkey and Iraq. The three mostly Kurdish areas are found in parts of the province of West Azerbaijan, the province of Kordestan (Kurdistan), and all of the province of Bakhtaran (formerly known as Kermanshah).

During the 1970s, many rural Iranian Kurds migrated from their villages to traditionally Kurdish cities such as Bakhtaran, Sanandaj, and Mahabad. Other Kurds settled in Iran's large non-Kurdish cities, such as Tabriz and Tehran. As a result, about two-thirds of Iranian Kurds now live in large towns and cities.

The ninth-largest city in Iran, with a population of almost 650,000, Bakhtaran is the capital of the province of the same name, which is the southernmost province in Iran. As an ancient city, it was named Kermanshah and was founded in the fourth century A.D. by the Sassanids. The Arabs captured the city in the seventh century, as did the Ottoman Turks during World War I. The name was changed from Kermanshah to Bakhtaran in 1979, at the time of the Islamic Revolution.

Bakhtaran is an important commercial center for agricultural products, such as grain, rice, vegetables, fruits, and oilseed, all of which come from the fertile lands of the surrounding region. The city is also an important manufacturing center, producing textiles and carpets; refined sugar and other processed foods; and refined petroleum.

> **The Kurds of Iran speak three major Kurdish dialects—Kermanji in Western Azerbaijan, Sorani in Kurdistan, and Gourani in Bakhtaran (spoken by the Hawraman tribe).**

Sometimes referred to as Iran's unofficial Kurdish capital, Sanandaj officially serves as the capital of the Kordestan province, in western Iran. Formerly known as Sinneh, Sanandaj is located in western Iran, close to the border with Iraq, and boasts a mostly Kurdish, Sorani-speaking population of almost 320,000. The city is Iran's 20th largest.

During the 19th century Sanandaj was the center for the production of Senneh *kilims,* finely woven carpets with bold bright designs crafted by Kurdish weavers. During the 1979 revolution, the city was also the scene of many battles between Kurdish rebels and the Islamic Revolution Guard. Sanandaj continues to be a site of Kurdish unrest.

Besides its famous *kilims,* Sanandaj and the surrounding region is also known for fine handicrafts such as woodwork, metalwork, and needlework. The city serves as a trade center for agricultural produce and features light industries such as textile manufacturing (carpets), tanning of hides and skins, rice milling, and sugar refining.

Located in West Azerbaijan, the historically Kurdish city of Mahabad served as the capital of the short-lived Kurdish nation of the same name, which was established in 1946. Almost 130,000 Iranians call Mahabad their home.

A large number of Kurds live on the outskirts of the Syrian capital, Damascus, in a section known as Hayy al Akrad (Quarter of the Kurds). Other groups live in the northeastern and northwestern parts of al-Jazirah and in the foothills of Kurd Dagh. Qamishli, located in the al-Jazira region, is home to a mixture of ethnic groups, including Kurds, Araqs, Turks, and Assyrians.

Kurdish demonstrators protest during a rally in Copenhagen, Denmark. The persecution that Kurds have endured in their traditional Middle Eastern homeland has forced many Kurds to immigrate to Europe, the United States, and other countries.

# 7

# *Foreign Relations*

Over the past century Kurds have appealed to foreign nations for help in obtaining civil rights in Turkey, Iraq, Iran, and Syria. Too often, Kurds say, when they have called upon the outside world, their requests have fallen on deaf ears. Many Kurdish people believe that history has shown an old Kurdish proverb to be true: "The Kurds have no friends but the mountains."

## *Kurds Around the World*

Exposure to Western ideas through the Internet and television has motivated many Kurds, especially young people, to search for a new life outside Kurdistan. Others have tired of living in areas where they cannot find jobs or where friends and family are jailed or killed for trying to speak in their native tongue. Subsequently, there has been a vast Kurdish *diaspora,* or scattering of people who have settled in regions far from their homeland. Approximately 800,000 Kurds live in Europe, with the majority (about 500,000) settled in Germany. Another 25,000 ethnic Kurds live in the United States and 6,000 in Canada. Although many Kurds have left the physical region of Kurdistan, they say the nation still lives in their hearts.

Some Kurds have left the region illegally, by working with human smuggling organizations that charge as much as $7,000 to smuggle immigrants into Europe. These arrangements simply involve setting up airline flights and helping with forged documents. Less expensive methods of leaving the country illegally are much more dangerous, and would-be immigrants often find themselves packed into the suffocating holds of trucks or boats with no food and little air. Those who risk leaving the country by crossing over the mountains during winter months face possible death from the harsh journey's freezing temperatures.

## Turkish Kurds and the European Union

The hundreds of thousands of Kurds living in European countries have been vocal in their criticisms of Turkey for its oppression of the nation's Kurds. And Europeans have exerted pressure on Turkey to make reforms since 1987, when the country first applied to become a member of the European Community (an economic organization of European countries that in 1992 became the political organization known as the European Union). In March 1995 Turkey was conditionally accepted into a customs union of the EU on the basis that it institute more democratic policies.

Soon afterward, the Turkish government's actions against the Kurdish rebels created further antagonism between Turkey and the EU. The Turkish government sent thousands of troops into northern Iraq to destroy

PKK bases. Tensions between Europe and Turkey remained high until the final Turkish military forces withdrew from Iraq a few months later.

The EU particularly criticized Turkey's treatment of Kurdish politicians. In 1994, seven Kurdish members of Turkey's National Assembly were arrested and charged with endangering national security. Four were sentenced to 15 years for "separatist speech," that is, advocating a separate Kurdish state.

Several European countries denounced Turkey for its lack of democratic methods in prosecuting the Kurdish deputies. Among the jailed leaders was one of the first women elected to Turkey's National Assembly, Leyla Zana. A dedicated activist for Kurdish rights, Zana was subsequently nominated by the Norwegian parliament for the Nobel Peace Prize in 1995, and again in 1998.

The European Court of Human Rights condemned the Zana trial in 2001, and three years later, as a result of reforms passed by the Turkish legislature to gain EU approval, the case went to retrial. An April 2004 decision by Turkey's State Security Court condemned the four Kurdish deputies to remain behind bars, casting a negative light on the government's progress regarding political reforms. However, the next month the Turkish government abolished the state security courts, and on June 14, 2004, an appeals court overturned the convictions of Zana and three other imprisoned Kurdish deputies. Following her release, she spoke in Kurdish before supporters, urging the PKK offshoot KONGRA-GEL to extend its ceasefire and utilize nonviolent tactics to gain rights for Turkish Kurds.

In 1998 the European Union had charged Turkey to make some drastic improvements in its treatment of the Kurdish people. The organization indicated that Turkey would not be considered for membership in the EU until the nation addressed its human right abuses. Turkey finally succumbed to the pressure, and in 2002 and 2003 the government approved laws granting more civil rights for Kurds. The arrival to power of a reformist political party,

**Former Kurdish deputies to Turkey's parliament Leyla Zana and Selim Sadak arrive in handcuffs at their retrial in Ankara, November 2003. European countries denounced Turkey for imprisoning Zana, the first Kurdish woman elected to the parliament, and other deputies in 1994. In June 2004, the sentences of Zana and three other deputies were overturned by the Turkish government.**

the Justice and Development Party (AKP), in November 2002, also had a major impact on the advancement of Kurds' rights.

Among the reforms was the approval of teaching Kurdish in schools. Private institutions in the cities of Van, Sanliurfa, and Batman attempted to start Kurdish classes, though bureaucratic hurdles caused delays. Kurdish broadcasts became legal in 2002, but the state-run television station TRT did not air a Kurdish-language program until June 2004.

# Iraqi and Turkish Kurds and the United States

Relations between Iraqi Kurds and the U.S. government have ranged from excellent to poor, as the United States has both supported and abandoned the Kurdish people. In the mid-1970s, the Iraqi Kurds felt particularly betrayed. At that time, Iraqi Kurds had approached U.S. leaders requesting help against Saddam Hussein's regime. At first the United States worked with the Kurds by providing military support through Iran. But then the pro-West leader of Iran, Shah Mohammad Reza Pahlavi, signed the Algiers Accord with Saddam Hussein, prompting the United States to change its policy. Because Iran was a U.S. ally and had come to terms with Saddam, the United States dropped its support of the Iraqi Kurds. Thousands were left to face the fury of Saddam as his Baathist forces entered northern Iraq and took vengeance on the rebellious Kurds.

The shifting alliances between Iran and the United States have further complicated matters involving Iraqi Kurds. In the early 1970s, the United States was allied with Iran and willing to go along with the decisions made by its government under the shah. However, by the end of the decade Iran's constitutional monarchy had been replaced by the Islamic Republic of Iran, a government that the United States strongly opposed.

Political alliances have also affected the Kurds living in Turkey. For many decades, U.S. leaders have considered Turkey a valuable ally. It is the only Muslim nation that is a member of the North American Treaty Organization, or NATO (a group of allied Western nations). Turkey was often looked to as a barricade against Saddam's regime in Iraq and, since the 1980s, the Islamic government of Iran. Accordingly, the U.S. government has not publicly criticized Turkey over Kurdish human rights violations or pressured its leaders to pass reforms that benefit the Kurds. In addition, the United States has stood by Turkey in its battles against

Kurdish rebels. Washington identified the PKK and its offshoots, KADEK and KONGRA-GEL, as foreign terrorist organizations, and has made promises to move against its members based in northern Iraq.

While the European Union's sympathy for the Kurds' plight is a source of comfort for the Turkish Kurds, many feel anger toward the United States for overlooking Turkey's repression of the Kurdish people. The Kurds of Iraq, on the other hand, have a positive attitude toward Americans, mostly because of the protection provided by the no-fly zone following the Persian Gulf War in 1991. They do not dwell on the betrayals of the 1970s and the inaction of the 1980s, when reports of Kurdish genocides in Iraq reached the leaders of the world's nations. At the time the United States and other Western nations did not respond either vocally or militarily against Saddam Hussein. Iran and Iraq were at war, and the United States had sided with Saddam Hussein because he opposed the Islamic Republic.

Kurdish leaders pressed the United Nations and Western governments after the massacres in 1983 and the *Anfal* campaign in 1988, pleading for action and support. But few believed the Kurds' claims that genocide was taking place in northern Iraq. It was not until 14 years after *Anfal* that Western nations accepted that the attacks had actually occurred.

## *Political Pawns*

The nations of Turkey, Iran, Iraq, and Syria have had shifting alliances among themselves, often because of issues related to the Kurds. At various times governments have gained advantage by playing the Kurds of neighboring countries against their governments. For example, a dispute with Turkey over the loss of the Hatay province in 1939 made Syria a long-time supporter of Turkey's Kurdish rebels, the PKK. After 1976, when Syrian troops occupied Lebanon, the PKK was permitted to run a training base there. And during the 1990s PKK leaders operated out of Damascus,

**After Saddam Hussein attacked the Kurds of northern Iraq in 1991, the United States and its allies established a "no-fly zone" over the northern part of the country, to prevent future aggression by the dictator. Here, an air force F-15 flies a routine patrol over snow-covered mountains in northern Iraq, 1999. The no-fly zone existed until the spring of 2003.**

Syria's capital. However, in a move to improve its relations with Turkey, Syria expelled the rebels in 1998.

Turkey and Iran had also been at odds before 1992. Turkey accused Iran of providing support to PKK rebels by allowing them to establish bases in Iran near the borders of the Turkish provinces of Kars, Agri, Van, and Hakkâri. But the establishment of the no-fly zone and the creation of the Kurdistan Regional Government concerned both countries. Iran believed that Iraqi Kurdistan had become a sanctuary for Iranian opposition groups, and in 1993 the Iranian government sided with Turkey in opposing the creation of any kind of independent Kurdish state in Iraq. Syria also declared the same belief that Iraq should remain intact as one nation.

# Effects of the 2003 Persian Gulf War

Following the 2003 war, Iraqi Kurdistan's neighbors looked to the region with great concern. The countries of Syria, Iran, and Turkey feared that the creation of a Kurdish state in Iraq would inspire Kurds in their countries to break away and form a separate nation. Turkey threatened to invade if Iraqi Kurds declared independence, and it insisted that the Kurds had no rightful claim to the oil-rich cities of Kirkuk and Mosul. The United States also opposed the breakup of Iraq, and instead supported the creation of a federal government in Iraq that would allow some autonomy in the northern region.

Of the three ethnic groups in Iraq, the Kurds had been most supportive of the U.S. action in Iraq, contributing *peshmerga* commandos and fighters to U.S. forces during the war and later in battles against insurgents. Most Iraqi Kurds welcomed the overthrow of Saddam, and unlike inhabitants to the south, felt no hostility to the fewer than 300 coalition troops that were based in Iraqi Kurdistan.

As violence in southern Iraq worsened in the spring of 2004, for the first time Turkey appeared to soften its opposition to a separate, autonomous northern Iraq. Some Turkish officials noted that Iraqi Kurdistan could serve as a buffer between Turkey and Iraq, whose active terrorist groups raised a serious threat. At the time Turkish companies were helping to build the airports, university campuses, and roads in Iraqi Kurdistan, and some Turkish officials were considering the benefits of offering protection to this economically sound region rather than opposing it. Turkey has since adopted a policy of cooperating with Iraqi political leaders.

An Iraq that remains united requires that Arabs, Turkmen, and Kurds, groups that for centuries have fought bitterly among themselves, live together in peace. The Iraqi Kurds' insistence on having control of oil-rich lands and maintaining a separate Kurdish militia complicates the likely success of an independence movement. But the Iraqi Kurds remain committed to their mission. In the spring of 2004, the *Wall Street Journal* noted that about 1.75 million Kurds had signed a petition demanding a referendum on Kurdish independence.

## A Divided People

Many political analysts believe that the Kurds have not been able to achieve power as a united ethnic group because tribal loyalty has stifled development of a Kurdish national loyalty. In the past, Kurds living in different nations have pledged allegiance to their regional tribes rather than to a united Kurdish nation. Turkish Kurds have fought Iraqi Kurds, who have fought Iranian Kurds.

This division has extended to how Kurds react to conflicts involving Kurdish groups and their respective governments. For example, Iraqi Kurdish leaders cooperated with the Turkish government in attempting to flush out PKK members based in northern Iraq. The PKK, in turn, has sharply criticized Iraqi Kurdish leaders and has promoted anti–Kurdish Regional Government propaganda through the pro-PKK television station, Medya. Such broadcasts have helped drive a wedge between the Turkish and Iraqi Kurds.

At times, the complex relationships among Kurds, opposition parties, and nations become a confusing puzzle. For instance, the government of Iran is said to support Ansar al-Islam, the radical Islamic group that has fought against the PUK. However, the PUK also has good relations with Iran, even

**Turkish riot policemen beat Kurdish demonstrators to disperse them from downtown Istanbul, where they were observing the anniversary of the 1988 Halabja massacre. Most of the people who attended this March 2004 demonstration were students or members of the Kurdish Democratic People's Party (DEHAP).**

though the PUK allows the Kurdish Democratic Party of Iran (KDPI), which opposes the Iranian government, to operate in northern Iraq. Iranian agents have also been granted permission to enter PUK territory in exchange for diplomatic, economic, and military aid from the Iranian government.

In addition to this environment of shifting alliances, significant language differences have divided Kurds in the past and continue to do so. One of the greatest problems remains the lack of a standardized written language, as Iraqi and Iranian Kurds use the Arabic alphabet while Turkish Kurds use the Roman.

In countries such as Iran and Turkey, where large numbers of Kurds have assimilated into their nation's respective societies, the Kurdish identity is no longer as strong as it used to be. In Turkey, many Kurds denied their origins to get ahead in business or the government, or to simply get a job. In both Iran and Turkey, many younger generations do not know how to speak Kurdish at all.

## Uniting Kurds with Technology

Around 1990, satellite television, which allows programs to be beamed all over the world, provided the first means for Kurds to share their message of nationalism with other Kurds, both inside Kurdistan and in Europe. A station licensed in Britain, the Kurdish Satellite Channel, brought the Kurdish language, map, and national anthem to Turkey and other parts of Kurdistan. Because such broadcasts were prohibited, Turkish government soldiers were sent out to destroy satellite dishes, and the Iranian government also protested against the broadcasts. But the satellite television network remained a powerful tool for spreading and strengthening Kurdish nationalism.

"I knew a family in Turkey," explained Kurdish researcher and University of Toronto professor Amir Hassanpour to Salon.com in April 2004. "They never believed they'd be able to see Kurdish on television, but when they saw the shows, they changed their mind. They believed the Kurdish nation could exist."

Today, language barriers are breaking down as television and radio announcers broadcast in Kermanji and Sorani. For about $100, Kurdish families can purchase a digital receiver and a satellite dish that provides access to Kurdish channels. Among the major television stations are the KDP's Kurdish Satellite TV, the PUK's Kurd Sat, and the PKK's Med TV, which broadcasts from Europe. A television set can be found in the homes of even the poorest Kurds.

Similarly, the Internet has allowed the culture of Kurdistan to grow in cyberspace. Kurds in different countries can talk with one another through weblogs and chat rooms. A variety of Kurdish websites educate Kurds and other people about the Kurdish language, history, music, and culture, as well as provide up-to-the-minute news coverage on issues of concern to Kurds. Many sites are named for the Kurdish nation, such as Kurdland.com, Kurdistan.net, and Kurdishmedia.com. Some media analysts refer to Kurdistan as a cyber-state—that is, a nation that exists online, if not in reality.

Through the Internet, Kurds in Turkey or Syria—countries that banned Kurdish publications—could get news of the progress of the fledgling government in northern Iraq. When Iraq's interim constitution was signed in

**Syrian President Bashar al-Assad (left) meets with new Iraqi Foreign Minister Hoshyar Zebari, who is a Kurd, in Damascus, March 2004.**

March 2004, with its guarantees of continued autonomy for Iraqi Kurdistan, Kurds in Iran and Syria celebrated with public rallies. Syrian demonstrators carried portraits of Kurdish leaders, notably Massoud Barzani of Iraq's KDP and Abdullah Öcalan, the jailed leader of the PKK.

That same month Internet reports about the clashes between Kurds and Arab police in Syria and reports of government violence against demonstrators quickly reached Kurds throughout the rest of the world. Many ethnic Kurds living in Europe and Iraq immediately took to the streets, demonstrating in support. Kurds in Iraq also marched in Arbil, where they called on the United Nations and human rights groups to end Syrian oppression of the Kurds.

Although they may not always understand each other's dialects, most Kurds believe they are united by their shared history of suffering and oppression. And as the Internet lifts barriers in communication—an issue that in the past has divided Kurds and reinforced tribal loyalty instead of national loyalty—Kurds may come closer to founding their own state. As the Internet gives Kurds around the world a way of connecting, it strengthens the nation of Kurdistan, making it an idea that could become a reality.

# *Chronology*

| | |
|---|---|
| **7th century** A.D. | Kurdistan is conquered and ruled by Arabs. |
| **Late 13th century** | The Ottoman Empire rules the Kurdistan region. |
| **1918** | British troops occupy the predominantly Kurdish and oil-rich Ottoman *vilayet* (province) of Mosul. |
| **1920** | The Treaty of Sevres that ends World War I dissolves the Ottoman Empire and promises the creation of the independent nation of Kurdistan. |
| **1923** | The Treaty of Lausanne supercedes the Treaty of Sevres and establishes Turkey as independent nation with claims to part of Kurdistan; the newly created nations of Iraq and Syria also include parts of the Kurdish homeland; Sheikh Mahmoud Barzinji incites uprising against the British, establishing Kurdish kingdom in northern Iraq that is overthrown by British forces the following year. |
| **1932** | A second Kurdish uprising, led by Mulla Mustafa Barzani and his older brother, Ahmad, is crushed. |
| **1943** | Mustafa Barzani leads another uprising and gains control over parts of Arbil and Badinan. |
| **1946** | Iraqi Kurdish rebels are defeated by the British, who drive them into Iran; Iraqi Kurds join Iranian Kurds, led by Qazi Mohamed, in establishing the independent Mahabad Republic, which falls in early 1947; the Kurdistan Democratic Party (KDP) is founded by Mustafa Barzani with the goal of creating an independent Kurdistan. |
| **1958** | The Iraqi monarchy is overthrown; a new Iraqi constitution promises Kurdish rights. |
| **1961** | Barzani leads northern Iraqi Kurds in revolt against the dictatorship of President Abd al-Karim Qasim. Although defeated, the Kurds continue sporadic fighting; Syrian census strips 200,000 Kurds of their citizenship. |

# Chronology

**1970**  Kurds are granted some self-rule and representation in Iraqi government.

**1974**  Disagreement over land issues results in the Kurdish Democratic Party's rejection of Iraqi government autonomy agreement; the KDP (with funding from the United States and Iran) attacks Iraqi government.

**1975**  Iraqi Kurdish uprising is crushed after the United States and the shah of Iran remove their support; Jalal Talabani breaks away from KDP and forms the Patriotic Union of Kurdistan (PUK).

**1978**  In Turkey, Abdullah Öcalan helps found the Kurdistan Workers Party (PKK).

**1979**  KDP leader Mustafa Barzani dies and is replaced by his son Massoud; Iranian Kurds revolt during Islamic revolution in Iran.

**1980–88**  Iraq begins war with Iran; Iraqi Kurds side with Iranian forces.

**1984**  Fighting breaks out in southeastern Turkey as Öcalan leads the PKK's armed struggle against the government.

**1988**  Towards the end of the Iran-Iraq war, Saddam Hussein's *Anfal* campaign results in the slaughter of thousands of Kurdish civilians and fighters, and the forced exile of another 1.5 million; thousands of civilians die in poison gas attacks on villages, including Halabja.

**1991**  A 34-member U.N. coalition enters into Persian Gulf War against Saddam Hussein; Kurds rise up against the Iraqi government at war's end but are crushed; coalition forces help refugees and set up no-fly zone in northern Iraq.

**1992**  Turkish military forces enter Iraq to attack PKK bases; elections are held in Iraqi Kurdistan.

| 1993 | Martial law is imposed in southeastern Turkey. |
|------|------------------------------------------------|
| 1994 | The two major Iraqi Kurdish political parties—the KDP and PUK—begin four years of fighting for control of the Kurdish autonomous region. |
| 1995 | Turkish troops enter Iraq to destroy PKK bases. |
| 1996 | KDP sides with Saddam Hussein's Iraqi army against PUK; U.N. oil-for-food program begins. |
| 1998 | PUK and KDP sign peace agreement. |
| 1999 | Öcalan is captured and convicted of treason by the government of Turkey; his death sentence is later reduced to life imprisonment; terrorist attacks follow his capture and trial. |
| 2001 | Fighting breaks out between the PUK and the Islamic fundamentalist group Jund al-Islam, later renamed Ansar al-Islam. |
| 2002 | Kurdish regional parliament reconvenes in Arbil after a six-year interruption. |
| 2003 | On March 20, U.S.-led coalition forces invade Iraq; in April, U.S. forces advance into Baghdad and take control of Kirkuk and Mosul with the help of Kurdish fighters; the U.S.-appointed Iraqi Governing Council (IGC), which includes several Kurdish leaders, meets in July. |
| 2004 | In February, more than 100 people, including senior political figures, die in suicide bombing at PUK and KDP offices in Arbil; Iraqi Governing Council approves interim constitution promising Kurdish autonomy for Iraqi Kurdistan; in June, the new Iraqi Interim Government, which includes a Kurdish vice president, replaces the Iraqi Governing Council. |

# Glossary

**arable**—suitable for farming.

**autonomous**—separate and under self rule, but not necessarily independent.

**caliph**—title for the religious and political leader of Muslims. In the Ottoman empire, the sultan claimed this position, but after the breakup of the empire the caliphate was abolished.

**crusade**—any war or campaign that is religiously motivated; the Crusades were military campaigns carried out by European Christians between the 11th and 13th centuries to take the Holy Land of Jerusalem from Muslim control.

**diaspora**—a dispersion of people who have left their homeland to live in other parts of the world.

**ethnic**—relating to a group of people who identify with one another on the basis of cultural or biological similarities, or both.

**embargo**—a prohibition on commerce.

*gecekondus*—shantytowns where the very poor live on the outskirts of Turkish cities.

**governorate**—an Iraqi government administrative province.

**mandate**—authority given by the League of Nations that its member nations administer and establish a government over territories taken from defeated empires after World War I.

**martial law**—the law applied in an occupied territory by military authority.

**nomad**—a person who has not settled in one location but moves from place to place seasonally and within a certain territory.

*peshmerga*—Kurdish guerrilla or independence fighters.

**plateau**—a relatively flat land area located at a high altitude.

**Qur'an**—the sacred book of Muslims, believed to be the word of Allah dictated to the prophet Muhammad by the angel Gabriel.

**Ramadan**—the ninth month of the Islamic calendar.

**shah**—a king or sovereign ruler of Persia or Iran.

**Shiites**—followers of the main minority sect of Islam; they believe the descendants of Ali (Muhammad's son-in-law) to be rightful heirs of the prophet Muhammad.

**steppe**—level, treeless, grassy plains that receive little rainfall.

**sultan**—ruler of the Ottoman Empire.

**Sunnis**—followers of the majority sect of Islam; they believe that the first four caliphs were the rightful spiritual and political leaders of Islam.

**vernal equinox**—the time during spring, around March 20 or 21, when the day and night are equal length.

# Further Reading

Bird, Christiane. *A Thousand Sighs, A Thousand Revolts: Journeys in Kurdistan*. New York: Ballantine Books, 2004.

Bodnarchuk, Kari J. *Kurdistan: Region Under Siege*. Minneapolis, Minn.: Lerner Publications, 2000.

Bulloch, John, and Harvey Morris. *No Friends but the Mountains: The Tragic History of the Kurds*. New York: Oxford University Press, 1992.

Chaliand, Gerard, ed. *A People Without a Country: The Kurds and Kurdistan*. Trans. Michael Pallis. New York: Olive Branch Press, 1993.

Davenport, John. *Saladin*. Philadelphia: Chelsea House, 2003.

Meiselas, Susan. *Kurdistan: In the Shadow of History*. New York: Random House, 1997.

### http://www.kurdistanweb.org/

Kurdistan Web provides links to a variety of information on Kurds and their heritage through maps, articles, and book excerpts on the history, culture, and language of the Kurds. It features links to the Encyclopaedia of Kurdistan Online.

### http://kurdmedia.com

Kurdish Media provides up-to-date news stories and information on Kurds and Kurdistan, as well as material concerning Kurdish language, art, and culture.

### http://www.puk.org/

Patriotic Union of Kurdistan's official site features background information on this major Kurdish political party in Iraq.

### http://www.kdp.pp.se/

The Kurdistan Democratic Party website provides information about this major Kurdish political party of Iraq, as well as links to additional information on Kurdistan's history and culture, Kurdish radio and television broadcasting, and the Kurdish Regional Government of Iraq.

### http://www.krg.org/

A source for news and background information on Iraqi Kurdistan and its Kurdistan Regional Government (KRG).

### http://www.dozame.org/

A place to find news stories and articles about Kurds within Turkey and in Europe.

### http://www.kurdishinfo.com/index.php?newlang=english

Another Internet source for news stories covering issues and events of interest to Kurds in Turkey and in the Kurdish diaspora.

# Index

Numbers in **bold italic** refer to captions.

# Index

# Picture Credits

The **FOREIGN POLICY RESEARCH INSTITUTE (FPRI)** served as editorial consultants for the GROWTH AND INFLUENCE OF ISLAM IN THE NATIONS OF ASIA AND CENTRAL ASIA series. FPRI is one of the nation's oldest "think tanks." The Institute's Middle East Program focuses on Gulf security, monitors the Arab-Israeli peace process, and sponsors an annual conference for teachers on the Middle East, plus periodic briefings on key developments in the region.

Among the FPRI's trustees is a former Secretary of State and a former Secretary of the Navy (and among the FPRI's former trustees and interns, two current Undersecretaries of Defense), not to mention two university presidents emeritus, a foundation president, and several active or retired corporate CEOs.

The scholars of FPRI include a former aide to three U.S. Secretaries of State, a Pulitzer Prize–winning historian, a former president of Swarthmore College and a Bancroft Prize–winning historian, and two former staff members of the National Security Council. And the FPRI counts among its extended network of scholars—especially its Inter-University Study Groups—representatives of diverse disciplines, including political science, history, economics, law, management, religion, sociology, and psychology.

**DR. HARVEY SICHERMAN** is president and director of the Foreign Policy Research Institute in Philadelphia, Pennsylvania. He has extensive experience in writing, research, and analysis of U.S. foreign and national security policy, both in government and out. He served as Special Assistant to Secretary of State Alexander M. Haig Jr. and as a member of the Policy Planning Staff of Secretary of State James A. Baker III. Dr. Sicherman was also a consultant to Secretary of the Navy John F. Lehman Jr. (1982–1987) and Secretary of State George Shultz (1988).

A graduate of the University of Scranton (B.S., History, 1966), Dr. Sicherman earned his Ph.D. at the University of Pennsylvania (Political Science, 1971), where he received a Salvatori Fellowship. He is author or editor of numerous books and articles, including *America the Vulnerable: Our Military Problems and How to Fix Them* (FPRI, 2002) and *Palestinian Autonomy, Self-Government and Peace* (Westview Press, 1993). He edits *Peacefacts*, an FPRI bulletin that monitors the Arab-Israeli peace process.

**LEEANNE GELLETLY** is a freelance writer and editor living outside Philadelphia. She has worked in publishing for more than 20 years and has written on a variety of subjects. Her books include the biographies *Harriet Beecher Stowe* and *Mae Jemison*; geography titles that explore Bolivia, Colombia, Somalia, and Turkey; and discussions of social issues such as Mexican immigration and violence in the media.